Romantic
WEDDING CAKES

Romantic WEDDING CAKES

KERRY VINCENT

MEREHURST

Contents

GUEST CAKES

Dedication

Born in the wheat-belt region of Western Australia, I spent most of my youth in rural Mt Many Peaks before moving on to Perth. Inspired by the daily theatre of jewel-like skies, fiery sunsets and pastoral life, I took my first tentative steps in the direction of creative art. Always curious and very single minded, little did I know that I would one day leave it all behind and embark on my own odyssey around the world. My life has been an amazing tapestry, moving from one magnificent country to the next, delighting in the strands of colourful cultural experiences that each has offered and weaving them into part of me. In the course of my journey through London I met my husband-to-be, American Douglas Lee Vincent, subsequently married him there and together we embraced a transitory lifestyle that continues to this day. Currently we reside in Tulsa, Oklahoma. My husband has supported me in the time-consuming endeavour of compiling this book, and I dedicate it to him. He has my heartfelt thanks for dealing so calmly with this interruption in our lives. This book is also a homage to the memory of my parents, Roy Henry Flynn and Dorothy Frances Flynn (née Farmer), neither of whom lived long enough to see how sugarcraft impacted my life, and to my parents-in-law, Swinford Jack Vincent aged 94 and Mabel Hulin Vincent (dec).

Wedgwood has had the privilege of supporting the Oklahoma State Sugar Art Show with the Wedding Cake Competition. This is the result of the talent and expertise of Kerry Vincent. Any book on the subject of Sugarcraft would be greatly enhanced by the involvement of Kerry Vincent.

The Lord Wedgwood

Acknowledgements

There have been many friends who have encouraged me along the path to sugarcraft – key personalities include Patricia Simmons (Australia); Pat Ashby, Jillian Cole, Gary Chapman and Sheila Lampkin (UK); and Maxine Boyington and Eileen Walker (USA).

None of this would have been possible without the incredible support of Gene Johnson (photographer extraordinaire) and his staff – Danny Le Grange. Lynnet Leigh and Scott Johnson at Hawks Photography.

Special thanks to Barbara Croxford for finding me, then choosing to work with me at such a disparate geographical distance. Together we proved it can be done.

Do You Take This Cake?

After my initial delight at being commissioned to produce a book on romantic cakes, I then thought long and hard about the approach I would take. It seemed to me that most existing books focused primarily on flower making. Although I love to make flowers – and they are an integral part of cake design – I decided that little attention had been seriously given to modern cake design. Since many sugarcrafters are expert at making beautiful flowers, I drifted into exploring display options.

At present the cutting edge for flamboyant style appears to be in the United States. There aren't any rules or regulations about what can or can't be done, so design has no limiting restrictions. Cake styling, though slow to change, always goes round in cycles, and each country has its turn at the top. Right now I believe there is a gentle upheaval in cake design. Every aspect of our lives is affected by fashionable trends: why not the cake? It has happened before, although slowly over the past centuries. The current love affair with cakes displaying drapes and lace is evident in all the major bridal magazines. Some purists are aghast at the amount of moulding being done at the expense of extension work and other more formidable techniques of the past. However, most of us are in the business of creating cakes for real brides for serious money, and the bottom line is that we must produce what they like and what they are willing to pay for. My cakes are very expensive and custom designed. There are no repeats under any circumstances. Not everyone wants to work this way: many like to work to a formula, providing a photograph album, catalogue style, so that the client can choose the basic design before making minor changes and colour variations. This keeps pricing simple, whereas I may be obliged to prepare a quotation after reviewing the bridal requirements.

Since I am the first person in the United States whom Merehurst has commissioned to write a cake decorating book, there has been a heavy sense of responsibility alongside this challenge. If I had failed to meet the criteria demanded, it would have closed doors for others, and my wish is to see talented United States cake designers given the opportunity to showcase their skills and ideas as I have done.

To my International Cake Exploration Societé friends both here in the United States and abroad, thank you for sharing and for challenging me. This book is for you to enjoy, turn the pages, be motivated, widen your decorative horizons, make magic and create something lovely. If that goal is realized, then I will have fulfilled my responsibility.

Finally, a portion of the proceeds from this book will be set aside to subsidize a scholarship to enable a financially strapped student to attend sugarcraft classes.

Kerry Vincent

Stylish Satin Sugar Roses

CAKE AND DECORATION

- 15 cm/6 inch, 20 cm/8 inch,
  25 cm/10 inch, 30 cm/12 inch
  and 35 cm/14 inch round cakes
- 1 kg/2 lb ivory flower paste/gum paste
- Antique silk lustre dust (VB/CK)
- 15 ml/3 tsp Tylose powder/CMC (J)
- 7 kg/14 lb ivory sugarpaste/rolled fondant
- Cornflour/cornstarch
- Moulded sugar vase (see pages 74–5)

EQUIPMENT

- 18-gauge wire
- Ivory floral tape
- Berling acanthus leaf mould (ADM –
  MPL 100)
- Kingston cutter formers (TOB)
- 8 cm/3 inch polystyrene/styrofoam ball
- 15 cm/6 inch, 20 cm/8 inch, 25 cm/
  10 inch and 30 cm/12 inch thin round
  cake boards
- 45 cm/18 inch round cake board
- Double scalloped crimper (PME)
- 100 mm/4 inch plaque cutter (J)
- Veining or Dresden tool (J or OP)
- 16 x 1 cm/$^1\!/_2$ inch dowel rods
- 17 x 5 mm/$^1\!/_4$ inch dowel rods
- Long sharpened dowel rod
- Matching fabric ribbon, to trim the
  45 cm/18 inch cake board
- Varipin/Rosa's Roller (OP)

A BRIDE CAN TRULY PERSONALIZE HER WEDDING WITH THESE LOVELY CLASSIC TIERS. GOWNS FEATURING WRAPPED RIBBON ROSES ARE VERY FASHIONABLE, SO IT IS A SIMPLE MATTER TO CUSTOMIZE THE CAKE TO MATCH. HER DREAMS ARE REALIZED WITH THIS IVORY CONFECTION — SO VERY MUCH IN TUNE WITH FASHIONABLE TRENDS, AND DELICIOUSLY BLENDING CLASSIC DESIGN WITH CONTEMPORARY OVERTONES.

SATIN FABRIC SUGAR ROSES

1 Roll out very thin pieces of ivory flower paste/gum paste to 5 cm/2 inches wide and in varying lengths, from 8 cm/3 inches to 10 cm/4 inches long. Brush a central strip, 2.5 cm/1 inch wide, with antique silk lustre dust. Fold each strip in half lengthways, and roll up loosely. Pinch it into a base, removing the excess paste.

2 Insert a dampened, hooked 18-gauge wire into the base of the rolled-up flower head. Tightly wrap the wire with ivory floral tape (pic 1), then dry for 2–3 days. This bouquet has 250 flowers. For fewer flowers or a smaller cake, shorten each flower stem. Rolled roses for the side design are not wired and should be made when required, because soft paste pushes into position more readily than pre-dried paste. Repeat step 1 for the unwired roses.

1 Wrapping the satin fabric sugar roses

HOW MOIST?

When attaching flower paste/gum paste and sugarpaste/rolled fondant to each other, remember that wet paste to dry paste is easy, as is wet to wet. The same, however, cannot be said for dry paste to dry paste, which can on occasion be quite resistant to gluing.

ACANTHUS LEAVES

3 To make the acanthus leaves, first add the Tylose powder to 500 g/1 lb ivory sugarpaste/rolled fondant. Knead well, then double wrap in plastic wrap and leave to rest overnight.

4 Lightly dust the acanthus leaf mould with cornflour/cornstarch. Roll out the paste thickly, then push into the mould. Run over the surface with a rolling pin. Cut across the mould surface, leaving the open-work effect exposed. Tease out the leaf with a knife (or freeze it briefly and it will pop right out – although this method is much more time-consuming). Brush with antique silk lustre dust, then lay the leaf on the Kingston former and dry overnight (pic 2). You will need 150 of these acanthus leaves.

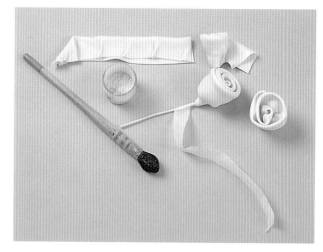

2 Making and drying acanthus leaves over the former

MAKING ACANTHUS LEAVES IN ADVANCE

Acanthus leaves are a useful side design for any cake and can be made well ahead in basic white paste. They nest easily, can be airbrushed any colour, occupy little storage space and are fabulous to have on hand to prepare an outstanding cake at short notice.

THE CENTREPIECE

5 Several days ahead, prepare the moulded sugar vase (see pages 74–5), making sure the centre is hollowed out sufficiently to accommodate the polystyrene/styrofoam ball. Decorate the sides with the stylized acanthus leaves. Brush the leaves with antique silk lustre dust while still damp. Cut the ball in half. Attach the half ball to the hollowed-out moulded sugar vase, using royal icing, and cover with a thin layer of sugarpaste/rolled fondant. Alternatively, dry a ball of sugarpaste/rolled fondant for two days, then insert in the same way. Arrange the flowers, spiralling down in even rows from the top to the bottom (pic 3).

PREPARING THE CAKES

6 Centre the cakes on the thin boards, then cover them and the 45 cm/ 18 inch board with ivory sugarpaste/rolled fondant. Crimp a row of double scallops at the upper edge of each cake. Emboss the upper surface of the top tier with the plaque cutter and veining tool (pic 4). Paint the embossed pattern with antique gold lustre dust mixed with clear alcohol.

3 Arranging the roses in the centrepiece

4 Quilted decoration and plaque

7 Stack the cakes one on top of the other, dowelling each tier before proceeding on to the next (see page 142). Hammer the long sharpened dowel through all five cakes, to stop shifting. Pipe a small royal iced border, to seal the cakes. Attach the acanthus leaf side design with royal icing, then the freshly made, rolled satin effect fabric sugar roses. Arrange for two people to carry the completed cake to the event, then add the centrepiece on-site.

ASSEMBLING THE CAKE ON-SITE

8 Alternatively, it can be stacked and decorated on-site. Leave a space free on either side for the offset spatulas. After centring, fill in the empty spaces with stylized acanthus leaves, then the roses. Pack the wrapped roses in plastic containers to keep them soft. Carry the centrepiece separately to the reception site. Pipe a ball of royal icing beneath the vase, and centre it on the cake.

This cake does not have as many steps as some of the other cakes and is well within the reach of an advanced beginner. It does take some time to prepare, however, because there are so many pieces. Tiers can be added or subtracted, according to event requirements. This cake will serve 230 people when made as a madeira or sponge/pound or white cake, comfortably reserving the top for the bride to keep for her first anniversary.

Sea Shades Shimmer

CAKE AND DECORATION

- 40 cm/16 inch oval cake
- 30 ml/6 tsp Tylose powder/CMC (J)
- 5 kg/10 lb sugarpaste/rolled fondant
- Green-gold, pale green, ruby, teal, avocado-green, coral, brown, yellow, antique silk, purple, super gold and bronze lustre dusts (VB/CK)
- 2.5 kg/5 lb caster/superfine sugar or granulated/regular sugar
- 310 ml/10 fl oz/1¼ cups water
- Pale blue, brown and yellow food colourings (VB/CK)
- 1 egg white

EQUIPMENT

- 40 cm/16 inch thin oval cake board
- Mylar, cardboard or paper template for the tropical fish (see page 152)
- Veining tool (OP or J)
- Various-sized drinking straws
- Round piping tubes/tips
- Paintbrush
- Varipin/Rosa's Roller (OP)
- 5 mm/¼ inch dowel rod
- Combination cutter veiner (RVO)
- Dusty miller cutter (RL)
- Rose leaf veiner
- Coral reef and shell samples
- Large glass or metal bowl
- Aluminium foil
- Sponge foam
- 45 x 5 cm/18 x 2 inch cake dummy
- Dressmaker's tracing wheel
- 65 cm/26 inch oval cake board

HERE, JEWEL-TONED TROPICAL FISH SWARM ABOUT A WHITE CHOCOLATE GROOM'S CAKE. THIS SOPHISTICATED SPIN ON THE TRADITIONAL VERSION IS CERTAIN TO PLEASE THE MOST DISCERNING OF TASTES. SEA THEMES AND SAND DUNES EVOKE THOUGHTS OF THE IDYLLIC PLEASURES OF A HONEYMOON TO COME.

PREPARING THE DECORATION MIXTURE

1 Knead the Tylose powder into 1 kg/2 lb sugarpaste/rolled fondant. Use this strengthened mixture for all the decorations on this cake. Set aside for an hour for the gum to dissolve, then knead once more.

MAKING THE TROPICAL FISH

2 Cut out a Mylar, cardboard or paper template for the fish (pic 1). Roll out the strengthened sugarpaste/rolled fondant and cut thirteen fish. Press the veining tool into the tails and the fins, to make sharp-pleated markings, and draw the paste out so it looks wavy. Using the various-sized drinking straws, the veining tool and the round piping tubes/tips, mark the scales, eyes and gills

1 Preparing the tropical fish

of the fish. Dust with green-gold, pale green, ruby and teal lustre dusts.

3 Prepare a little paste mound with the veining tool, indenting the centre where the fish will be positioned. Cut three small slits where the coral and sea grass will be inserted. Set aside for a couple of days to firm up.

2 Making the coral tubes and sea grass

CORAL AND SEA GRASS

4 Make the hollow underwater coral tubes from various-sized strips of strengthened sugar paste/rolled fondant embossed with the Varipin/Rosa's Roller and wrapped around the thin dowel rod. Press down hard to seal the join, then colour with avocado-green, coral and pale green lustre dusts (pic 2). Set aside to dry.

5 Meanwhile, cut out the long sea grass from the strengthened sugarpaste/rolled fondant, using the combination cutter veiner. Immediately brush with pale green, teal and brown lustre dusts. Curl the tops over, then dry flat.

CORAL REEF AND SHELLS

6 The dusty miller cutter is an excellent cutter to substitute for coral. These pieces are also cut from the strengthened sugarpaste/rolled fondant, veined with a rose leaf veiner or a rose leaf from the garden, then shaded with coral, yellow, antique silk and purple lustre dusts. For the reef moulds, simply collect two or three samples from the seashore or buy them from hobby craft shops. Press them into the strengthened paste. Freeze briefly to set the shape, then dry hard for a week or two. The original reef pieces, the mould and the moulded piece are quite hard to tell apart (pic 3). They can be white, marbled or dusted.

7 For the shells, roll out the strengthened paste and press on to the back of a natural shell. Peel away, trim with a craft knife or scalpel, and brush with antique silk, super gold and bronze lustre dusts.

3 Coral reef and shell collection

TROPICAL BACKGROUND ASSEMBLY

8 Streak some royal icing with pale blue food colouring. Using a palette knife and the blue-streaked icing, ice/frost the little mound so that it resembles sea waves. Position the fish into the centre of the mound while the icing is wet. Add some foam support until dry. Meanwhile, push in the coral and sea grass. Prop everything until the icing is set hard.

BEACH SAND

9 Colour the remaining sugarpaste/rolled fondant so it resembles beach sand, using yellow and brown food colourings.

ROCK SUGAR

Rock sugar is fun to make and very realistic. Preheat the oven to 120°C/250°F/GM½. Line a large glass or metal bowl with the foil. Combine 1 kg/2 lb caster/superfine sugar or granulated/regular sugar with 250 ml/8 fl oz/1 cup water in a large saucepan – the sugar eventually doubling in size. Stir over low heat, taking normal precautions when boiling sugar, such as removing any scum accumulating on the top and brushing any sugar granules down from the sides of the pan. When dissolved and beginning to boil, partially cover the saucepan and bring the sugar to 124°C/255°F. If colouring is required, add it now. Continue boiling until the temperature reaches 140°C/275°F. Remove from the heat source and immediately stir in 30 ml/2 tbsp royal icing. Beat lightly; do not overbeat. The mixture will puff up like a meringue, fall a little, then rise again. For more porous rock sugar, add extra royal icing.

Immediately pour into the prepared bowl and put in the oven for 10 minutes, to set the sugar. Remove from the oven and leave for 10 hours. Chop or break it into pieces for your project – a serrated knife works best. Rock sugar lasts for ages and can be lightly airbrushed once the pieces are set in place.

MOULDED SUGAR

10 Mix together the remaining caster/superfine sugar or granulated/regular sugar, remaining water and the egg white. Substitute albumin powder, if you wish.

CAKE ASSEMBLY

11 Attach the cake with royal icing to the thin cake board. Centre the cake on the cake dummy and cover both with the beach sand sugarpaste/rolled fondant. Draw some vertical accent lines around the cake with the tracing wheel and brush with super gold lustre dust. Pile the moulded sugar on to the 65 cm/26 inch cake board using a palette knife like a trowel to pack it down and smooth the surface. Centre the cake on this board. Pipe a walnut-sized ball of royal icing in the centre of the cake, then stand the sea grass and hollow pipes upright within it. Crumble a little rock sugar over the icing so it can't be seen. Prop with sponge foam until dry.

12 Arrange three fish in a tight triangle around the grass, attaching them to the top of the cake with royal icing and surrounding them with shells. Circle the cake with individual ornamental fish and dot the moulded sugar with coral, shells and rock sugar.

Pintucks and Pansies

CAKE AND DECORATION

- 20 cm/8 inch, 25 cm/10 inch and 30 cm/12 inch scalloped oval cakes
- Yellow, moss-green and purple petal dusts (VB/CK)
- 85 g/3 oz pale lemon flower paste/gum paste
- Purple food colouring
- Purple lustre dust (VB/CK)
- 7 g/¼ oz moss-green flower paste/gum paste
- Sugar crystals, from Chinese food stores
- Hi-lite orange lustre dust (OP)
- 6 kg/12 lb pale lemon sugarpaste/rolled fondant
- Moulded sugar vase (see pages 74–5)

EQUIPMENT

- 20- and 28-gauge wires
- Paper templates for pansy petals (see page 152) or large rose petal cutter (OP – R1)
- Ball tool • Dried cornhusk
- Medium five-petal blossom cutter (such as OP – F2L, or PME)
- Mid-green floral tape
- Leaf cutters (OP – OL2, OL3, OL4)
- Veining or Dresden tool
- Natural leaf veiner • Dimpled foam mat
- Polystyrene/styrofoam ball
- 20 cm/8 inch, 25 cm/10 inch and 30 cm/12 inch thin oval cake boards
- 38 cm/15 inch scalloped cake board
- Open scalloped crimper
- 13 x 5 mm/¼ inch dowel rods
- Long sharpened dowel rod
- Fluorescent light cover pattern
- Lace mould cutters (RVO – F13 and F11)
- No.000 piping tube/tip
- Daisy centre moulds (J)
- Dressmaker's tracing wheel
- Sponge foam

SOUTACHE ACCENTS WITH PINTUCKS AND PANSIES EPITOMIZE THE VERY ESSENCE OF A SPRINGTIME WEDDING. SIGNATURE EFFECT IS CREATED WITH HUGE PURPLE AND PARCHMENT PANSIES. FEMININE SUGAR STREAMERS POOL GRACEFULLY ON THE CAKE BOARD. ADDED HINTS OF PURPLE AND GREEN IN A DRIFT OF LEMON SOUFFLÉ WOULD MAKE THIS CAKE A SUPERB HIGHLIGHT AT ANY WEDDING DAY!

THE PANSIES

1 For the central stamen, make a tiny ball of white flower paste/gum paste just large enough to support the very large pansy petals. Tinge with yellow and moss-green petal dusts and attach to the 20-gauge wire.

2 Roll out the pale lemon flower paste/gum paste and cut the petals using the template or rose petal cutter. Ruffle the edges with the side of the ball tool (pic 1). Vein the petals with the dried cornhusk. Place them on a petal pad, starting at the top of the flower and descending – right/left top petals, then right/left side petals, centre and finally the bottom petal. Touch each overlapping corner with edible gum glue and press together,

1 Creating pretty pansy faces

making sure each makes contact. Press the stamen through the centre of the flower as well as a piece of supporting aluminium foil, then set aside to dry over a glass. Paint in the dark markings with purple food colouring mixed with clear alcohol/vodka or Everclear. When dry, brush lightly with purple lustre dust.

3 Make a Mexican hat with six points from moss-green flower paste/gum paste, for the calyx. Hollow out the base, thin the edges and insert the pansy wire. Tip with a little edible gum glue. Make a blossom cutter frill and attach with edible gum glue. Wrap the stem with mid-green floral tape.

2 Sets of leaves in progress

3 Preparing sugar crystals

THE LEAVES

4 Cut out sets of leaves in moss-green flower paste/gum paste, using all the leaf cutters. Thin the edges and increase the width of the leaves by stretching with the veining or Dresden tool. Brush with moss-green petal dust and vein the surface with the leaf veiner. Insert 28-gauge wires, then wrap with floral tape (pic 2). Lay the leaves on the dimpled foam mat to dry.

SUGAR CRYSTALS

5 Brush each crystal with hi-lite orange and purple lustre dusts (pic 3). Use the crystals to support the flowers and foliage and to conceal the polystyrene/styrofoam ball.

PREPARING THE CAKES

6 Centre the cakes on matching sized thin cake boards, which have been scalloped to shape and covered with contact paper. Cover each cake and the banded, 38 cm/15 inch, scalloped cake board in pale lemon sugarpaste/rolled fondant, so it matches the pansy colour. (A small amount of yellow kneaded into

PANSY CUTTER OPTIONS

The pansies on this cake are particularly large, measuring 10 x 8 cm/4 x 3 inches. For these, use the pansy petal templates (see page 152) or a large rose petal cutter such as OP R1, although the rose petal cutter will not produce the same size. You might therefore need to adjust the decoration by making an extra flower, should this latter option be adopted. It is, however, faster to work with the cutter.

white paste is close to the colour of the natural flower and looks like lemon soufflé.) Before the surface crusts, crimp the scalloped pattern vertically into the four recessed areas of each cake, using the open scalloped crimper, and circle the cake board with the same pattern. Paint the centre of the crimped scallops with hi-lite orange lustre dust mixed with clear alcohol/vodka or Everclear. The next day, centre the bottom cake on the covered cake board, securing with royal icing.

7 Insert seven dowels 8 cm/3 inches in from the edge and follow the contour of the bottom cake (see page 142). Stack the middle tier on top and insert six dowels 8 cm/3 inches from the edge. Add the top tier after placing a blob of edible gum glue between it and the previous tier. Hammer the long central dowel through all the cakes, to stop shifting during transportation. Add double-row swags, starting and ending at the centre of each recess.

SIDE DESIGN

8 Now comes the fun part. Emboss the rolled out sugarpaste/rolled fondant with the fluorescent cover pattern. Using the small set of lace mould cutters for the top and middle tiers, and the larger set for the bottom tier, lay the embossed paste over one of the lace moulds and shallow cut. (Please note: I did not push the paste right down into the cutter moulds, because a different personalized pattern was the goal.) Lay on the tabletop and coax the pieces into the shapes shown (pic 4), one piece being cut in half vertically. Outline each piece with running dots, using the piping tube/tip, and brush immediately with hi-lite orange lustre dust.

9 Form the pattern by building out from the centre lace points (pic 5). (It doesn't have to match this one exactly – allow your imagination to take flight and create an

4 Creating the soutache pieces

individual masterpiece.) Attach each piece to the cake sides with edible gum glue. Cut up additional pieces to fill empty spots and make sure whatever happens on the right-hand side is repeated on the left. The back of the cake is a replica of the front. Make a range of different sized buttons in sugarpaste/rolled fondant, using the daisy centre moulds. Add these buttons in graduating

5 Stages of the lace mould process

sizes at join points, to pull the effect together – it is the key to the design work. Also cover the joins in the double-row swags with the largest buttons. Brush the buttons with hi-lite orange lustre dust.

BOW LOOPS AND STREAMERS

10 Press thinly rolled sugarpaste/rolled fondant on to the sheet of fluorescent light cover pattern, embossing the surface. Cut into a curved pointed shape (pic 6), following the template on page 152. (This template can be sized up or down to suit any cake dimension.) Turn the paste sides under, then 'stitch' along the edges with the tracing wheel. Pleat at the top and run the tracing wheel down the top end of the pleat, to form pintucks. Brush with hi-lite orange lustre dust and attach to the side of the cake with edible gum glue. There are two overlapping panels on each side and these are also repeated at the back. Add four pleated open loops, once again 'stitching' the pintucks into position with the tracing wheel before layering and attaching with edible gum glue. Finally add a fifth loop, placing it vertically (pic 7); support in position with sponge foam until dry. Cover the join with a small pleated knot.

FINISHING OFF

11 Cut four stylized leaves, long oak or something similar to the cutter shown (pic 8), in the embossed sugarpaste/rolled fondant. Following the contour of the leaf, press in

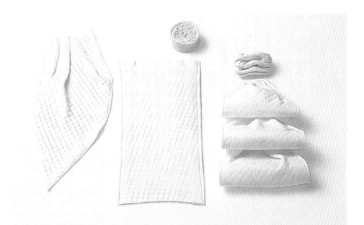

6 Bow loops and streamers

8 Satin leaves and cutters

edging dots using the piping tube/tip. Brush with hi-lite orange lustre dust and tuck the leaves under the knot, securing with edible gum glue.

12 Cover the moulded sugar vase in sugarpaste/rolled fondant and decorate with lace soutache. Circle the vase base and the rim with a thin rope, and insert styrofoam, securing it with edible gum glue. Leave for at least a day, until the glue has dried, before adding and arranging the flowers and foliage; otherwise the arrangement could topple.

7 Attaching the fifth loop

Pêche Belle La Russe

CAKE AND DECORATION

- 15 cm/6 inch, 20 cm/8 inch and 30 cm/12 inch round cakes
- 2.75 kg/5 lb 10 oz pale peach sugarpaste/ rolled fondant
- 30 g/1 oz balls of green, dark peach, purple and pale blue sugarpaste/rolled fondant
- Pale green, mauve, silk-white and super gold lustre dusts (VB/CK)
- 30 g/1 oz pale green flower paste/gum paste
- 125 g/4 oz/¹/₂ cup peach caster/ superfine sugar
- 15 ml/1 tbsp alcohol-flavoured, simple syrup for each bonbonière/favour

EQUIPMENT

- 100 mm/4 inch plaque cutter (J)
- Medium and large maple leaf cutters (RL)
- Natural insecticide-free rose leaf
- Selection of four different blossom cutters
- Veining tool
- Small and medium-sized half-ball sugar moulds (PME)
- Carnation cutters (OP – C1 and C2)
- Ball tool
- Berling acanthus leaf mould (ADM – MPL 100)
- Kingston cutter former (TOB)
- Plunger cutters (PME or OP – F2M and F2L)
- Broderie anglais cutter (PME)
- 15 cm/6 inch and 20 cm/8 inch thin round cake boards
- 38 cm/15 inch round cake board
- Large single scalloped crimper (PME)
- Brocade lace mould (ELI)
- Satay stick/bamboo skewer
- Parsley cutter or sharp knife
- 8 x 5 mm/¹/₄ inch dowel rods
- Bun tins/gem cake pans

TODAY'S CAKE STYLISTS ARE THROWING TRADITION TO THE WIND AS BRIDES OPT FOR MORE TRENDY, CUTTING-EDGE DESIGNS. WHITE HAS ALWAYS BEEN THE OBVIOUS CHOICE BUT MODERN BRIDES ARE NOW ABANDONING TRADITION AND CHOOSING WEDDING CAKES IN EVERY COLOUR OF THE RAINBOW. THIS COUTURE-INSPIRED CAKE DESIGN IS MEANT FOR THE ROMANTIC AT HEART.

1 Plaque cutter and maple leaves

VINCENT MARQUETRY TOP PLAQUE

1 Cut out a plaque from 60 g/2 oz of the pale peach sugarpaste/rolled fondant, using the plaque cutter. Immediately cut out three maple leaves in two sizes, and replace them with the same leaf, in green paste. Vein the leaves with a natural insecticide-free leaf. Then overcut two more leaves, one of each size (pic 1). Brush with pale green dust.

2 Using the selection of blossom cutters and 30 g/1 oz each of the dark peach, purple and pale blue sugarpaste/rolled fondant, cut into the leaves, replacing the discarded scraps with solid-coloured flowers – the more overcutting, the prettier the design. Press in a throat with the veining tool (pic 2). Brush the purple flowers with mauve lustre dust, and the others with silk-white lustre dust. Paint the plaque edge with super gold lustre dust mixed with alcohol. Paint flourishes, extending out from the spray. Make four feet from moulded sugar, using the small half-ball mould. Position under the plaque.

VINCENT MARQUETRY

Generic Vincent Marquetry plaques can be made months ahead and stored. They are extremely useful to have on hand for short-notice occasions, and are a great way to recycle coloured remnant sugarpaste/rolled fondant and flower paste/gum paste.

2 Inlaid plaque with flowers and cutters

3 Carnation petals and cutters

CARNATIONS

3 Cut four rounds using the medium carnation cutter. Frill the edges and place the first three on top of each other, to make the flower. Press the centre with the ball tool, forcing the petal sides upwards. Fold the fourth piece into an S-shape and insert at the centre of the flower (pic 3). Repeat this method, using the small carnation cutter. You will need thirty-two carnations of each size.

MAPLE LEAVES

4 Prepare pale green, rose-veined, flower paste/gum paste maple leaves, with the maple leaf cutters and natural rose leaf veiner. Brush with pale green lustre dust (pic 4). Fold each leaf in half, to attach to the cake border beneath the carnations on the top and middle tiers. The remainder should have the sides lifted slightly before slipping beneath the flowers on the top and bottom tiers. While still damp, attach the leaves to the cake with edible gum glue or royal icing.

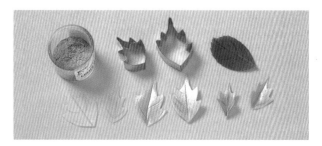

4 Making the maple leaves

ACANTHUS LEAVES

5 Press firm pale peach sugarpaste/rolled fondant into the mould. Cut away the excess with a very sharp knife, then shave the top away carefully, leaving the cutwork exposed (pic 5). Immediately remove the leaf from the mould, or freeze it briefly. (Freezing stops the medium from stretching and makes it easier to remove.) Brush the leaves with silk-white lustre dust, then dry over the shaped former. Twenty-four of these acanthus leaves will be required, but make a couple of extras in case of breakages.

FILLER FLOWERS

6 Make the filler flowers from the purple and dark peach sugarpaste/rolled fondant, using the large plunger cutter (pic 6). Cut out peach blossoms with the medium-sized plunger cutter and the Broderie anglais cutter. After attaching, pipe in a single stamen in white royal icing.

PREPARING THE CAKES

7 Dampen and sprinkle the 38 cm/15 inch cake board with the peach caster/superfine sugar. Place the top and middle tier cakes on matching-sized thin cake boards. Cover the three cakes with sugarpaste/rolled fondant. Centre the bottom cake on the sugar-covered cake board. Working from the bottom cake upwards, embellish the upper edge of each tier with the scalloped crimper. At the junction of each space, push in a single, medium-sized peach blossom, and finish with a piped white stamen.

BOTTOM TIER

8 Mark the edge of the lace mould 10 cm/4 inches from the base. Using this as a guide to ensure uniformity of depth, roll out the sugarpaste/rolled fondant. Press into the lace mould with a foam

5 Stylized acanthus leaf side design

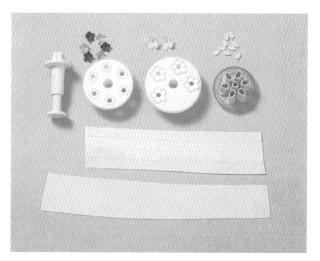

6 Filler flowers and matching cutters

sponge. Brush the raised design with silk-white lustre dust. Form into pleats with a satay stick/bamboo skewer (pic 7), and glue to the cake side, tucking the last pleat under the first, so there is no visible join.

MIDDLE TIER AND TOP TIER

9 Using royal icing, attach the acanthus leaves and carnations to the middle tier, followed by the leaves and filler flowers. Measure the circumference of the top tier and divide the cake in six. Using the parsley cutter or sharp knife, cut strips of thinly rolled sugarpaste/rolled fondant the depth of the top tier cake, then brush with silk-white lustre dust.

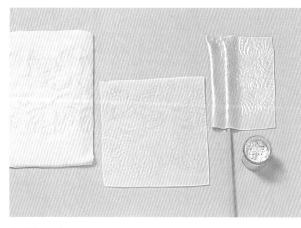

7 Pleats in progress

Matching bonbonières/favours look spectacular whether displayed with the cake or served individually

8 Decorating bonbonières/favours

Attach these strips with the minutest amount of water. Cover each of the rough edges at the top with a single blossom. Attach the carnations and leaves at the lower edge, using royal icing.

STACKING THE TIERS

10 Put four dowels each into the bottom and middle cakes (see page 142), extending the dowels 2.5 cm/1 inch above each cake. Prepare eight moulded sugar half-balls, with holes in the centre, using the medium-sized, half-ball mould. Slip one over each dowel to disguise the wood, and glue them to the cake surface, using royal icing.

11 For transportation, sit each tier on a larger cake board with non-skid rubber matting. Stack the tiers at the reception. Touch each dowel top with a blob of royal icing and, using an offset spatula, lift each cake into position. Add the cake top plaque, and line the carnations up with the paste ribbon strips.

BONBONIÈRES/FAVOURS

Make the cakes in bun tins/gem pans. When completely cool, drizzle with the alcohol-flavoured, simple syrup, then cover with sugarpaste/rolled fondant. Divide each cake evenly. Cut eight 5 mm/ 1/4 inch strips of paste and brush with silk-white lustre dust, then attach to the cake (pic 8). Attach the maple leaves, acanthus leaf, medium carnation and filler flowers with royal icing, in the order given.

Mosaic Magic

CAKE AND DECORATION

- 15 cm/6 inch, 20 cm/8 inch, 25 cm/10 inch, 30 cm/12 inch and 35 cm/14 inch round cakes
- 250 g/8 oz white flower paste/gum paste
- Purple and green powdered food colourings (VB/CK)
- Sifted white polenta/cornmeal
- Green, super gold, silk-white and brown lustre dusts (VB/CK)
- Larkspur, pale blue, white and yellow petal dusts (VB/CK)
- 7.5 kg/15 lb pale cream sugarpaste/rolled fondant (75:25 white and ivory mixed)
- Moulded sugar vase (see pages 74–5)

EQUIPMENT

- Paper templates (see pages 152–3)
- Ball tool
- Large needle
- Shallow celformer, pierced through the base
- Long thin calyx cutter from a hibiscus or rose cutter set
- 20- and 26-gauge wires
- Tiny five-petal flower cutter
- 18 x 0 line brush
- Leaf veiner
- Rose leaf cutter
- Piece of rippled foam
- Floral tape
- 15 cm/6 inch, 20 cm/8 inch, 25 cm/10 inch, 30 cm/12 inch and 35 cm/14 inch thin round cake boards
- 45 cm/18 inch round cake board
- Grosgrain ribbon, 1.5 mm/⅝ inch wide, to trim 45 cm/18 inch cake board
- Adding machine tape
- Dowel rods (see page 142)
- Textured rolling pin (EC)
- No.10 piping tube/tip (W)

MOSAIC ART HAS BEEN AROUND FOR CENTURIES. ARTISTICALLY PLEASING TO THE EYE, IT IS A TIMELESS TECHNIQUE TO CELEBRATE A COLOURFUL WEDDING. GOLDEN CONFETTI SHARDS AND LUSTROUS PEARL TILES ARE PLACED IN INTRICATE PATTERNS CREATING EXOTIC SIDE DESIGNS, WHILE HYDRANGEAS PEEP OUT BENEATH AMETHYST BALLOON FLOWERS CLUSTERED IN A STUNNING CAKE ORNAMENT.

WIRED BALLOON FLOWERS

1 Mould a marble-sized ball of flower paste/gum paste. Roll out the edges, leaving it very thick in the centre. Using the template (see page 153), cut out the star-shaped, balloon flowers. Brush heavily with purple powdered food colouring. Remove excess. Press firmly with the ball tool and hollow out the centre, so the sides of the stars begin to cup. Thin the edges of the petals and pierce the centre with a large needle, then rest in the celformer.

2 Prepare a small, inner, tube-shaped circle. Cut even little nicks into the surface and dust with purple and green powdered food colourings. Position over the needle hole in the centre of the flower.

3 With the long thin calyx cutter from the hibiscus or rose cutter set, trim the stamens to a very thin star shape (pic 1). Roll each of the five points between the thumb and forefinger. Run a thin paint line of edible gum glue along each point and sift white polenta/cornmeal over the top. Make the stigma thin, dark purple and bottle shaped. Attach a hooked 26-gauge wire to it, then push through the flower centre. Dampen the join with edible gum glue. Add a tiny five-petal flower on top of the stigma. Paint dark vein lines on the petals with the line brush, using purple food colouring mixed with clear alcohol/vodka or Everclear.

1 Balloon flowers coming to life

2 Balloon flower: stages of calyx and buds

BACK OF THE FLOWER AND BUDS

4 The calyx is a simple five-point star with a small, elongated hip beneath. Make the buds in the same way, eliminating the flower centre (replace with a hooked wire and a pea-sized ball of paste) and close the petals (hence the balloon shape) so the centre cannot be seen (pic 2). Colour them lighter than the flowers, using purple food colouring brushed with green lustre dust. Close the petals to meet evenly in the front and to a point. The pattern is exactly the same, although smaller for the bud.

HYDRANGEA FLOWERS

5 These have anywhere between three- and five-petal combinations. Attach tiny balls of flower paste/gum paste to the 20-gauge wire, cut in 15 cm/6 inch lengths. Twelve hours later, cut out the petals in paste, using the hydrangea flower template. Thin the edges with the ball tool. Press with the leaf veiner. Arrange in the celformer, overlapping each petal. Carefully push the wired centre through and attach with edible gum glue. Dry for 24 hours before touching. Brush with larkspur, pale blue and white petal dusts with a spot of yellow at the centre (pic 3). For the side design, use the same pattern, method and colouring – no wire, of course.

3 Hydrangea petals and flowers

FOLIAGE

6 Prepare the leaves with the rose leaf cutter. Then offset the cutter again, slicing a bit off each side. Wire the leaf. Vein the surface and lay on a piece of

4 Rose leaves trimmed to size

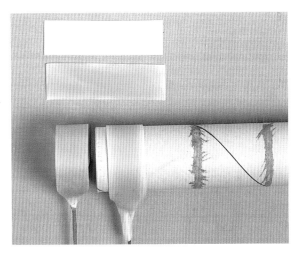

5 *Shaping gold ribbon loops*

rippled foam to dry. Floral tape the wires. Attach the leaves on one side of the stem only, then position immediately beneath each other, graduating from small to large (pic 4). For the side design, use the same method, pattern and colouring but omit the wire and remove the oblong piece to insert the stem.

GOLD RIBBON LOOPS

7 Dry 20-gauge wired, 2 cm/³/4 inch strips of super gold-brushed flower paste/gum paste formed in a circle over a kitchen paper towel roll (pic 5). Tape all wires when the flowers and ribbons are absolutely dry.

7 *Balloon flowers in the side design*

> ### MOSAIC DESIGN
> The same mosaic design is repeated on the top, third and bottom tier cakes. For added interest, the second and fourth tier cakes feature complementary patterns.

MOSAIC TILES

8 Roll out strips of flower paste/gum paste and cut in 5 mm/¹/4 inch squares with a craft knife or scalpel (pic 6). While still soft, brush with silk-white lustre dust. Do not separate until required – it will be easier to match the pieces. For the brown strips, prepare some thin oblong pieces by cutting each tile in quarters. Brush with brown lustre dust.

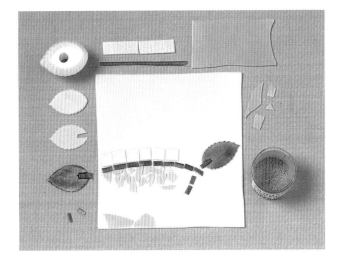

6 *Placing the mosaic tile pattern*

Dry thoroughly, then snap apart. Keep the colours separated. For the gold pieces, prepare long strips of thin paste. Dust with super gold lustre dust while the paste is wet. When dry, break into small pieces. (If required the pieces can be made larger than those used here – the decorating will then go much faster.)

TOP, THIRD AND BOTTOM TIER SIDE DECORATION

9 Cover each cake with the pale cream sugarpaste/rolled fondant. Divide the cakes into eight even sections and arrange the white tile outline. Roll out some flower paste/gum paste and cut out more balloon flowers. Dust with purple food colouring. Paint darker purple vein lines with the line brush, using purple food colouring mixed with clear alcohol/vodka or Everclear (pic 7). Add a thin calyx stamen topped with the mini star-shaped blossom at the centre. Dust with sifted white polenta/cornmeal. Attach the flower to the cake sides with

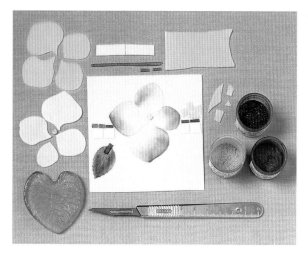

polenta/cornmeal. Attach the flower to the cake sides with edible gum glue. Add the hydrangea petals and green leaves. Fill the remaining space with gold pieces (pic 8).

SECOND AND FOURTH TIER SIDE DECORATION

10 Divide the cake measurement into repeat sections by folding the adding machine tape. Cut a wavy line duplicating the pattern provided on page 153. Mark the design on the cake. Glue the tiles around the top border. Glue the blossoms and foliage into position. Add more tiles and brown strips. Fill with the gold pieces.

8 Hydrangea flowers in the side design

ASSEMBLY

11 Stack the cakes, dowelling each tier (see page 142). For the hollow tubes, emboss some paste with the textured rolling pin. Wrap around the long scrap dowels. Press down to seal (pic 9). Slide off into position on the cake and cover each join with a single tile.

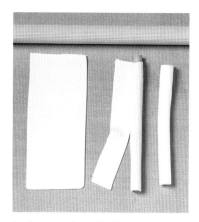

9 Stages of the hollow tubes

FLORAL CENTREPIECE

12 Prepare the moulded sugar vase (see pages 74–5). Remove an ice-cream scoop-sized ball from the centre. Once dry, fill with a round ball of sugarpaste/rolled fondant and set aside for several days. Decorate the exterior with a simple mosaic pattern. Arrange in the following order: gold ribbon loops, wired balloon flowers, hydrangea flowers and rose leaves.

A TOUCH OF ELEGANCE

Why not make tiny gift tags to match the wedding cake and place them on the serviettes at the table of honour? (It would not be advisable to suggest making these for all the guests, as they are a bit fiddly and time consuming.) Duplicate parts of the main design on to small flower paste/gum paste rectangular plaques. Punch out a round hole with the piping tube/tip. Using the other end as a cutter, cut out two round disks. Remove the centres with the same tube/tip so all the holes match. Line up on the plaque and join with edible gum glue. Fill in the mosaic pattern, then thread a strip of paste ribbon through the hole.

How Sweet it is – Cake for Two

CAKE AND DECORATION

- 8 cm/3 inch and 10 cm/4 inch round cakes
- 750 g/1^1/$_2$ lb white sugarpaste/ rolled fondant
- 60 g/2 oz pale pink sugarpaste/rolled fondant
- 15 g/^{1}/$_2$ oz pale pink flower paste/ gum paste
- Orchid-pink, super pearl and cornflower-blue lustre dusts (VB/CK)
- Larkspur, lime-green and moss-green petal dusts (VB/CK)

EQUIPMENT

- 8 cm/3 inch and 15 cm/6 inch thin round cake boards
- Small double scalloped crimper (PME)
- China cake or dessert plate
- 4 x 5 mm/^{1}/$_4$ inch dowel rods
- Medium flower cutter (PME – plunger or medium blossom)
- Mini leaf cutter
- Grosgrain textured rolling pin (EC)
- Dressmaker's tracing wheel
- Sponge foam
- Petal pad (OP)
- Dresden tool
- Veining tool
- 8 cm/3 inch diameter carnation cutter (J)
- Celformer (CC)
- Soft medium paintbrush
- Aspic bird cutter
- 18 x 0 line brush

A PRETTY PINK PORCELAIN-LIKE CAKE AS FRESH AS A SUMMER BREEZE AND READY TO ACCOMPANY THE BRIDE AND GROOM ON THEIR HONEYMOON. OFTEN OVERWHELMED BY THE EXCITEMENT OF THE DAY, THE BRIDAL COUPLE HAVE LITTLE TIME TO REALLY ENJOY THEIR RECEPTION CAKE, SO SUGGEST MINIATURE TIERS FROM THE MAIN CAKE DESIGN, BEAUTIFULLY BOXED, FOR LATER.

CAKE PREPARATION

1 Place the top tier cake on the 8 cm/3 inch cake board. Trim the board with a craft knife or scalpel, if necessary, so the diameter is slightly less than the cake. Cover the cake with sugarpaste/rolled fondant right down over the edges of the board. Also cover the bottom tier cake with paste, while it is on a temporary board.

2 Cover the 15 cm/6 inch thin cake board with sugarpaste/rolled fondant. Embellish the edges with the double scalloped crimper. Attach sugar grosgrain ribbon to the edge of the board (see step 3). Centre the cake board on the china cake plate, and glue with royal icing. One day later, gradually ease a palette knife under the bottom cake and lift into position at the centre of the cake board. Custom measure, then cut and insert the dowels (see page 142). Add the top tier.

CAKE BASE DECORATION

3 Measure the base of each cake, then add an extra 1 cm/½ inch. Cut two 3 cm/1¼ inch wide strips of sugarpaste/rolled fondant by the expanded circumference measurement, and emboss with the flower and leaf cutters. Brush the flowers with orchid-pink lustre dust and larkspur dust. Using lime-green dust, tint the flower centres and leaves (pic 1), and attach to each cake base. Remove overlapping paste. Emboss pink sugarpaste with the textured rolling pin. Cut 5 mm/¼ inch strips and attach a strip above and below the floral side panels with gum glue, then brush with super pearl.

1 Embossing the band

THE BOW

4 Prepare the offset bow with pale pink sugarpaste/rolled fondant, using the same embossing technique as for the cake base. Cut two ribbon tails, each 13 x 15 cm/5 x 6 inches. Run the tracing wheel along the longer, base edge, to simulate stitching. Fold the sides under and gather the top edge. Cut 13 x 8 cm/5 x 3 inch strips from the remaining embossed paste, for the ribbon bow loops. Fold under the sides and pinch in the raw edges (pic 2). Attach the tails and bow loops to the cake, with the royal icing or edible gum glue. Support the bow pieces with sponge foam. To give a sense of movement, add some strips of sugar grosgrain ribbon, guiding them to follow the drape of the bow, then prop them up. Position the bow centre, and accent the edge with grosgrain ribbon.

2 Making an embossed bow

DECORATING THE CAKE BOARD

5 Using the flower cutter, cut out the blossoms from sugarpaste/rolled fondant. Place on a petal pad. Thin the edges with the Dresden tool, and press in the centre throat, using the veining tool. Turn the flowers upside down to dry in shape, or use a commercial drying rack. When dry, pipe a tiny dot of white royal icing into the flower centre and tint with orchid-pink lustre dust (pic 3). Attach to the cake board, with royal icing. Cut out the leaves with the leaf cutter. Brush with moss-green petal dust and attach in position with a water-dampened paintbrush.

3 Sets of flowers and leaves for cake board embellishment

4 Making the large carnation

CARNATION PREPARATION

6 Cut ten layers of petals from pale pink flower paste/gum paste, using the carnation cutter, and place under plastic wrap, to prevent drying out. Using a craft knife or scalpel, cut nicks into the petal edges, and ruffle them with the Dresden tool. Brush them with a combination of orchid-pink and cornflower-blue lustre dusts, adding tints of lime-green petal dust (pic 4). Partially dry the petals in a shallow celformer. Stack each layer on top of the other, propping with foam to separate. When the space at the top becomes very small, fold the final round in half, then in quarters/fourths, forming an S-shape. Fit into the space and tease the ruffled edges evenly with a soft paintbrush. It may be necessary to clip a little off the base, for uniform height. Attach to the top of the cake with royal icing or gum glue, and allow to dry.

5 Birds take flight

THE BIRD

Create a small bird in the flower paste/gum paste, using the bird cutter. Brush with orchid-pink lustre dust. Mix a little of the orchid-pink lustre dust with clear alcohol/vodka or Everclear, and paint tiny dots on the body with the fine paintbrush (pic 5). Attach to the cake with a tiny dot of royal icing. Paint an orchid-pink lustre dust flourish beneath the bird, and another trailing away behind it.

Picture Perfect Couture Cake

Cake and Decoration

- 15 cm/6 inch, 25 cm/10 inch, 35 cm/ 14 inch and 40 cm/16 inch round cakes
- Small, round, moulded sugar vase (see pages 74–5)
- 750 g/1¹/₂ lb flower paste/gum paste and sugarpaste/rolled fondant in a 50:50 mixture
- 7 kg/14 lb champagne-ivory sugarpaste/ rolled fondant
- Super gold and antique silk lustre dusts (VB/CK)

Equipment

- Small jar
- Daisy button mould (J)
- Rose garland stencil – with small and large graduated pattern (CSD)
- Scallop-edged broderie anglais cutter (PME)
- 20-gauge wire
- White floral tape
- Sponge foam
- 15 cm/6 inch, 25 cm/10 inch and 35 cm/14 inch thin round cake boards
- 50 cm/20 inch round cake board
- Double open-scalloped crimper (PME)
- Veining tool
- Paintbrush
- Electric pasta machine (optional)
- Satay sticks/bamboo skewers
- 14 x 1 cm/¹/₂ inch dowel rods
- 5 x 5 mm/¹/₄ inch dowel rods
- Double-sided lace mould (ELI)
- Varipin/Rosa's Roller (OP)
- Rose leaf cutters (OP – R6 and R6A)
- Cardboard former
- Long sharpened dowel rod

GLEAMING WITH GOLDEN HIGHLIGHTS, THIS GRACEFUL CAKE DUPLICATES THE LUSTRE OF FINE SILK. A DISTINCTIVE LAYERED OVER-SKIRT CASCADES FROM TIER TO TIER IN PERFECT SYMMETRY. GILDED, COILED ROSETTES ARRANGED IN A FRAGILE FLOUNCED VASE ADD ROMANTIC FLAIR TO THIS SPLENDID DECORATIVE DESIGN. MAGICAL SUGAR WITH A MIDAS TOUCH.

VASE PREPARATION

1 Prepare a moulded sugar vase (see pages 74–5), hollow out the centre and allow to dry. Turn the vase upside down on a small jar and attach two gathered panels of stencilled 50:50 flower paste/gum paste and sugarpaste/rolled fondant mixture, hiding the joins in overlapping folds and gluing the seams. Make bisque daisy buttons, and attach at the base. After drying overnight, carefully return to the upright position. Press a golf ball-sized piece of sugarpaste/rolled fondant into the hollowed-out, moulded sugar vase. Dry overnight.

FANTASY FLOWER ROSETTES

2 Prepare the large flower rosettes for the centrepiece from the 50:50 mixture by stencilling the paste with the small stencil pattern. Cut two lengths, full width, with the broderie anglais cutter, pleat and circle each length into a rosette. Join the ends with edible gum glue, and insert the wire. When dry, wrap the wire with white floral tape.

3 To form the smaller rosettes, use just half the width of the broderie anglais cutter (pic 1). Proceed as above, without the wire. Make daisy button centres, dust with super gold, then add to all the flower rosettes (pic 2). Dip the flower stems in royal icing/buttercream; arrange and support them in the vase.

1 Paste cut to full and half widths by the broderie anglais cutter

PREPARING THE CAKES

4 Place all the cakes except the bottom tier on matching-sized, thin cake boards. Centre the bottom tier on greaseproof/waxed paper and place on a temporary cake board. Cover the 50 cm/20 inch round cake board with sugarpaste/rolled fondant, allow to crust overnight, and centre the bottom tier on it. This is easy to do by sliding the cake across from one board to the other, while pulling the greaseproof/waxed paper. Cover the cakes with paste, bringing it over the board edges. Form a pretty edge with the double scalloped crimper. Also crimp within the circle on the top tier. Add extra interest with the side of the veining tool. Paint the raised centre of the crimped edge with super gold lustre dust mixed with clear alcohol/vodka or Everclear.

MAKING THE GATHERS

5 Measure the circumference of each cake and divide by five, marking the places to ensure accuracy when placing the swags later. Working on the bottom tier first, roll out the mixture of flower paste/gum paste and sugarpaste/rolled fondant. Cut out 9 x 30 cm/3¹/₂ x 12 inch

2 Fantasy flowers coming together

sheets – using an electric pasta machine will save time (see page 143). If long pieces seem daunting, shorten the lengths.

6 Measure the depth of each tier and mark the rose garland stencil accordingly, to help keep the pattern repeat level. Press the paste sheet into the large rose garland stencil pattern, using a sponge. Turn over and brush with super gold lustre dust. Carefully remove the panel, then lay flat. Gather evenly, using satay sticks/bamboo skewers, then press down firmly at the top and glue to the cakes. Continue overlapping the panels until the last, which should be slipped under the first, forming a continuous skirt. Repeat for the second and third tiers, using the smaller rose garland stencil (pic 3).

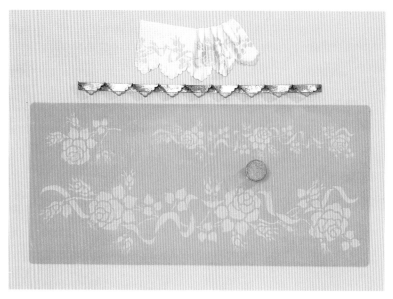

3 Rose garland stencils and short gathers

SUGGESTIONS FOR THE BRIDE

This cake was designed to be built in individual tiers, depending on the number of servings required. The top tier alone would serve about seventy-five guests with fruitcake but only sixteen if prepared with madeira or sponge/pound or white cake. As the guest list grows, add extra tiers. The visual effect will not be compromised.

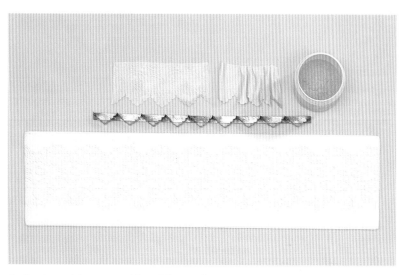

4 Embossed lace, mould and lustre dust

5 Stencilled swag ready to attach

STACKING THE CAKES

7 Using seven 1 cm/$1/2$ inch dowel rods each for the bottom and third tier and five 5 mm/$1/4$ inch ones for the second tier, push in a circle of dowel rods, to support the cakes when stacked (see page 142). Stack each ascending tier after inserting the dowels. Completely decorate each tier before adding the next.

LACE FLOUNCES

8 The top tier has two gathered rows of embossed lace. Roll out sheets of champagne-ivory sugarpaste/rolled fondant. Press into the lace mould with a dry sponge. Remove carefully. Cut into 30 x 8 cm/12 x 3 inch strips and brush with antique silk lustre dust (pic 4). Gather panels using a satay stick/bamboo skewer and attach to the side of the cake, with edible gum glue. Attach the first level of flounce at the centre of the cake and the second to the top, so they overlap. Add a dollop of buttercream or royal icing between each tier, to stop sliding. Paint the edges with super gold lustre dust and clear alcohol/ vodka or Everclear.

THE SWAGS

9 Stencil the swags, using the small pattern on the rose garland stencil. Graduate the lengths, according to the measurements taken on each cake, and fold the sides under (pic 5). Add the swags, taking care to line them up evenly. Paint the edges of the skirt with super gold lustre dust mixed with clear alcohol/vodka or Everclear. Experiment with the mixture to be sure it is thick enough to be visible – if there is too much alcohol, the edging will have no impact.

FABRIC-EFFECT LEAVES

10 Texture some sugarpaste/rolled fondant with the Varipin/Rosa's Roller. Cut the leaves in two sizes, with the rose leaf cutters. Brush with super gold lustre dust and attach immediately, using a slightly water-dampened paintbrush. Leave a few textured leaves to dry over the cardboard former (pic 6), to add extra

6 Textured leaves curled over the former

interest to the shape. Using royal icing, attach the dried leaves on the top tier, so the leaves curl back towards the centre of the cake. Centre a fantasy flower and leaves on each join where the swags meet.

FINISHING

11 Measure and hammer the long sharpened dowel through the three assembled tiers. Nip the top so the dowel does not protrude above the paste, using pruning shears kept specifically for this job. Keep the top tier separate and slip it on at the reception site, adding a little blob of royal icing under the board for security. Finally add the centrepiece.

SERVING SUGGESTIONS

If the completed cake is three tiers or more, pack the top tier and centrepiece separately and attach it at the reception site. Arrange for two people to carry the dowelled cake. When the cake is to be cut, break away the side decorations with a chef's knife before cutting to serve. Remember that the long lace mould is double sided, and the reverse was used for the side design on Pêche Belle La Russe (page 21). This is indeed excellent mileage from one product.

Valentine's Heart Sublime

CAKE AND DECORATION

- 30 cm/12 inch heart-shaped cake
- 175 g/6 oz white flower paste/gum paste
- 30 g/1 oz moss-green sugarpaste/rolled fondant
- 3.5 kg/7 lb white sugarpaste/rolled fondant
- Super pearl lustre dust (VB/CK)
- 125 g/4 oz white flower paste/gum paste and sugarpaste/rolled fondant in a 50:50 mixture

EQUIPMENT

- Medium blossom cutter (OP – R2)
- Gardenia cutter set (NL)
- Veining or Dresden tool
- Sponge, for support
- Paper templates for gardenia leaf (see page 153)
- Leaf veiner
- 38 cm/15 inch cake board
- Varipin/Rosa's Roller (OP)
- Greaseproof/waxed paper
- Medium daisy button mould (J)
- Lace mould (SB – 8N395)
- Shallow, slightly curved dish
- Brocade cutter mould (RVO)
- Make-up sponge
- Dressmaker's tracing wheel

THERE IS NO MISTAKING THE MESSAGE THIS SUGAR-CLAD HEART EVOKES — AFFECTION, FLIRTATION AND LOVE'S PROMISE. THIS SWEET TREAT IS ENHANCED WITH A SINGLE GARDENIA TRIMMED WITH SATIN BIAS AND LOVELY TOUCHES OF LACE. SHINING WITH HIGH GLOSS PEARL, A SIMPLY CUT BOW WITH STREAMERS WRAPS AROUND THE SIDES OF THE HEART. PURE BLISS FROM CUPID'S CAKE STYLIST DEAR VALENTINE!

THE GARDENIA

1 Cut two sets of small white flower paste/gum paste blossoms with the medium blossom cutter, for the flower centre. Thin the edges and curl one side only inwards on each petal (pic 1). Furl into a rosette, then wrap the second set around the first.

2 Cut the small set of gardenia petals, and thin the edges. Run the veining or Dresden tool around the outer edge, forcing the petals upwards. Turn the petals back to the right side. Make two more petal sets, but with the larger gardenia cutter. Layer the petals by offsetting them and attaching with edible gum glue. Twist to add some movement and shape, then prop into position with the sponge. Finally add the rosette centre.

1 Gardenia whorls and leaves

FOLIAGE PLATE

3 Using the gardenia leaf template (see page 153), cut the four-point leaf 'plate' from moss-green sugarpaste/rolled fondant. Emboss each segment with the leaf veiner, pinch the tips together and set aside to dry flat. Glue the completed gardenia flower into the centre of the leaf.

PREPARING THE CAKE

4 Cover the cake board with white sugarpaste/rolled fondant and texture the surface edge with the Varipin/Rosa's Roller, then set aside to dry. Meanwhile position the cake on greaseproof/waxed paper. Paint a little edible gum glue into the centre of the prepared cake board. Cover the cake with white sugarpaste/rolled fondant and slide on to the cake board. Carefully trim the greaseproof/waxed paper.

BANDS AND SCALLOPS

5 For the continuous 'bias' bands at the base of the cake, cut three 90 x 10 cm/36 x 4 inch strips of white sugarpaste/rolled fondant. Attach with edible gum glue, beginning and ending at the centre back of the cake. Trim neatly, and brush with super pearl lustre dust. Cover the join with medium rounded buttons, made from paste using the daisy button mould.

6 Divide and mark each cake side in three even scallops, using a scalloped arc. Angle each one slightly down to the front. Cut 15 x 2.5 cm/6 x 1 inch strips of white sugarpaste/ rolled fondant and brush with super pearl lustre dust. Fold in half and coax into a gentle curve, then glue to the cake, following the scalloped arc.

LACE DECORATION

7 To make the side decoration, brush the inside of the lace mould with super pearl lustre dust. Roll out a thick piece of the white flower paste/gum paste and sugarpaste/rolled fondant paste mixture. Press into the mould, cover and press firmly with a rolling pin. Remove the excess paste, tidy the edges, then freeze. Remove from the mould, and cut out the accent eyelets. Attach to the cake side, slightly overlapping the scallop decorations. Fill any spaces between joins with little lace pieces. Done carefully and with thought, the lace decoration will appear seamless.

8 For the top, prepare three more lace pieces, keeping one flat for the top of the cake, at the front. Place the other two in the shallow, slightly curved dish, to dry (pic 2). Attach securely at the back of the cake, with the gardenia centrepiece placed between.

2 Curved lace decoration with bands and scallops

BROCADE

9 Roll out fairly thin, very firm flower paste/gum paste. Brush the brocade cutter mould with super pearl lustre dust, then press the paste into the mould with a make-up sponge. Roll across the cutting edge with the rolling pin, then remove the piece from the mould. Lay flat to dry. Fit these brocade pieces end to end around the edge of the board and cake top, attaching with edible gum glue.

THE BOW

10 Cut three 20 x 10 cm/8 x 4 inch strips of white sugarpaste/rolled fondant. Diagonally trim the tails of two strips, then turn the side edges under all of them. Brush with super pearl lustre dust, and run the dressmaker's tracing wheel along the edge of each, to simulate stitching (pic 3). Position the bow tails on the back of the cake and drape across the board slightly, curving around the edge of the cake and attaching with edible gum glue. Split the remaining strip evenly, then fold in half and cut in the centre. Pinch the ends together and attach with edible gum glue at the back of the cake. Cover the join with a gathered and glued knot of super pearl-dusted, white flower paste/gum paste.

3 Putting the bow together

Romancing the Dome

CAKE AND DECORATION

- 15 cm/6 inch, 20 cm/8 inch, 30 cm/12 inch and 40cm/16 inch round cakes
- 7 kg/14 lb pale ivory sugarpaste/rolled fondant (50:50 white and ivory mixed)
- 125 g/4 oz white flower paste/gum paste
- 30 g/1 oz moss-green flower paste/ gum paste
- Super pearl and avocado lustre dusts (VB/CK)
- 10 ivory roses (see pages 94 and 119)
- 10 blue hydrangeas (see page 28)
- Buttercup petal dust (VB/CK)

EQUIPMENT

- 15 cm/6 inch polystyrene/styrofoam ball
- 15 cm/6 inch, 20 cm/8 inch and 30 cm/12 inch thin round cake boards
- Two 40 cm/16 inch round cake boards
- 45 cm/18 inch round cake board
- Ivory ribbon, to trim cake board
- Pale blue dupioni silk
- Parsley cutter
- Lace rose mould (SB – 8F955)
- Medium paintbrush
- Rose leaf cutter (OP – R5)
- Natural or commercial rose leaf veiner
- Sliver leaf cutter (RVO)
- Plunger cutters (PME or OP – F2M and F2L)
- Pointed-tipped large blossom cutter (RL)
- Ball tool
- Large tea rose cutter (PC)
- Checked stencil (CSD)
- Satay stick/bamboo skewer
- Dowelling (see page 142)
- Daisy button centre (J)
- Long sharpened dowel

IMPERIAL DOMES CROWN MOST OF THE GREAT CITIES OF THE WORLD. THEY HAVE ALWAYS REMINDED ME OF THE ULTIMATE WEDDING CAKE. OUT OF A SOFT SUMMER SKY COMES THIS ROMANTIC INTERPRETATION. IMPOSING CAKE LAYERS ARE TRIMMED WITH RICH RIBBON TAPES AND CHECKED SATIN PLEATS. CREAMY WHITE TEA ROSES AT THE SIDE ARE ACCENTED BY DAINTY BLUE HYDRANGEAS.

PREPARING THE CAKES

1 Cut the polystyrene/styrofoam ball in half and attach with royal icing to the 15 cm/6 inch thin round cake board. Cover each cake with pale ivory sugarpaste/rolled fondant and centre the top three tiers on identically sized thin round cake boards. Glue two 40 cm/16 inch cake boards together and attach the pale blue dupioni silk to the 45 cm/18 inch cake board, using spray adhesive. Make sure each board is very secure before adding the cake. Centre the bottom cake on the board, using royal icing as the gluing agent.

THE DOME AND TOP TIER

2 Centre the dome on top of the upper tier and glue together with a generous spoonful of royal icing or buttercream. Measure the depth of the ball and the depth of the top tier cake, then divide the circumference into eighths.

3 Prepare 5 mm/¼ inch strips of sugarpaste/rolled fondant with the parsley cutter, and attach eight pairs to the surface of the dome and the cake sides. Cover the joins at the dome top with the moulded lace rose, brushed with super pearl lustre dust (pic 1). Using the double strips of ribbon as the centre guide, decorate an inverted 'V' of tiny, small and medium blossoms and foliage.

1 Moulded rose dome accent

2 Stages of rose and miniature leaves

FOLIAGE

Make large rose leaves from moss-green flower paste/gum paste, using the rose leaf cutter, then vein them with a natural or commercial rose leaf and brush with avocado lustre dust (pic 2). Dry fairly flat before attaching between the second and third tiers. Attach one leaf on each side of where a rose will sit, using royal icing. Make tiny pale ivory leaves with the leaf sliver cutter or cut them freehand; brush with super pearl dust and attach with royal icing.

FLOWERS

The template and instructions for hydrangea flowers are given on pages 28 and 152, and for the rose on page 94. Attach the hydrangeas between the rose leaves, then sit the roses on top. Make the flowers for the dome and decorative accents elsewhere with the plunger cutters and the pointed-tipped large blossom cutter (pic 3). Having cut them out, soften the edges and press in the centre throat with the ball tool. Attach to the cake with royal icing or push directly into the cake.

3 Making hydrangea and filler flowers

THE SECOND TIER

4 Measure the depth of the second tier plus 8 cm/3 inches, and cut 5 mm/¼ inch strips with the parsley cutter, then brush with super pearl lustre dust. Extend the ribbons 8 cm/3 inches over the top and down over the cake sides, and attach. This cake needs seventy strips.

THE THIRD TIER

5 Very thinly roll out the white flower paste/gum paste and drape over the cutting edge of the large tea rose cutter. Press in gently with a sponge (pic 4) and leave to stand for a minute to set, then turn right side up and cut down. Let the paste remain in the cutter for another minute, then turn out on to the work surface.

6 When fairly firm, brush with super pearl lustre dust (pic 5) and highlight the rose with buttercup petal dust. Without disturbing the puffed effect, attach immediately to the side of the third tier. At the top and base of the rose appliqué, add three medium blossoms.

4 Pressing paste into the cutter

5 Dusting the appliqué roses

6 Adding lustre before forming the pleats

THE BOTTOM TIER

7 Cover the dupioni silk on the 45 cm/18 inch cake board with plastic wrap before making the pleats. Roll out the sugarpaste/rolled fondant and press on to the checked stencil. Brush with super pearl lustre dust. With a light touch, cut 15 x 15 cm/6 x 6 inch square panels while still on the stencil. Peel away and form into uniform pleats with the satay stick/bamboo skewer (pic 6). Attach the panels to the bottom cake with gum glue (see page 143).

HOLLOW TUBE DECORATION

8 Measure the spaces between the paired paste ribbons in the top tiers. Stencil thin strips of paste, using the checked stencil (pic 7). Form around the dowel, pressing down to close the join. Cut and attach a tube between the ribbons. Make daisy button centres to cover the joins on all the tiers.

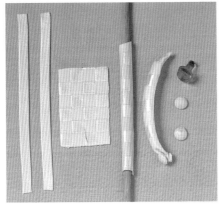

7 Stages of the hollow tube decoration

ASSEMBLY

9 Dowel (see page 142) and stack the three lower cakes for transportation. Add the top tier at the reception. This cake will be very heavy, so, if the cake stylist is delivering alone, box the tiers separately. Pack the roses and prepare the hollow tubes and daisy centres at the last minute, cover with plastic wrap and seal in a plastic container. Attach the hollow tubes, leaves, hydrangeas and roses with royal icing when the cakes are finally assembled on the table of honour. Alternatively, instead of the hollow tubes, simply pipe borders around the cakes.

Tiers in a Teacup

CAKE AND DECORATION

- 8 cm/3 inch round cake, 5 cm/2 inches deep
- 5 cm/2 inch round cake, 4.5 cm/1¾ inches deep
- 2.5 cm/1 inch round cake, 3 cm/1¼ inches deep
- 500 g/1 lb sugarpaste/rolled fondant
- Super gold lustre dust (VB/CK)
- Gold highlight powder (VB/CK)
- Pale blue, lavender, yellow and pale green food colourings
- Rubine and cerise petal dusts (OP)
- 55 g/2 oz flower paste/gum paste
- Moss-green and pale lemon petal dusts (VB/CK)

EQUIPMENT

- Plastic drink coaster or lace doily
- 10 cm/4 inch cake board
- Shell tool (J)
- 2 x tiny foil-covered thin round cake boards
- Three-piece tea set
- Satay stick/bamboo skewer
- Posy mould (SB – 4662)
- 18 x 0 line brush
- Miniature rose leaf cutter (OP – R16)
- Tiny flower cutters (RVO)
- Small centre from the Garrett frill set (OP – GF3) or round paper template (see page 153)
- Oval paper template (see page 153)
- Ovate, pointed leaf cutter (RVO)
- Medium blossom cutter (OP – F2L)
- Veining tool
- Quilting pin
- Electric pasta machine (optional)

TINY TIERS PERCHED ON TEA-SET PLACE SETTINGS MAKE AN ALTERNATIVE CHOICE TO THE RECEPTION WEDDING CAKE. WEAVING NEW TRENDS INTO AGE-OLD TRADITION, SOME COUPLES ARE NOW OPTING FOR THESE DRAMATIC INDIVIDUAL DESSERTS. CREATE YOUR OWN TINY TEACUP CAKES, MATCHING DIFFERENT PATTERNS TO SEASONAL OCCASIONS, AND LET YOUR DESIGNER SPIRIT FLY.

PREPARING THE CAKES

1 Emboss some sugarpaste/rolled fondant with a lace pattern, using the plastic coaster or doily (pic 1). Cover the cake board with lace-embossed paste. Paint with super gold lustre dust and gold highlight powder mixed with clear alcohol/vodka or Everclear. Bind the edge with a strip of sugarpaste/rolled fondant and emboss with the shell tool. Centre the paste-covered bottom cake on the board.

2 Make a foil-covered, thin round cake board for the middle tier a smidgen smaller than the cake's diameter, and another for the top tier. Position each cake on the appropriate board. Colour some sugarpaste/rolled fondant to match the tea set, although this may prove difficult because the colour of white china and porcelain varies tremendously – some having a really creamy cast while other varieties look quite blue. Kneading in the tiniest touch of blue was a good choice for the colour match here. Cover the cakes, bringing the paste right down over the edge of the foil-covered boards. Stack the cakes, putting a little dab of royal icing or buttercream between each tier. Push a satay stick/bamboo skewer through the centre of all three. Clip off flush with the top.

1 *Lace-embossed paste covering for the cake board*

2 *Moulding the miniature floral centrepiece*

FLORAL CENTREPIECE

3 Prepare the miniature flower centrepiece, using the posy mould (pic 2). Paint the predominant flowers with rubine and cerise petal dusts mixed with clear alcohol/vodka or Everclear. Using the line brush, decorate the remaining flowers with lavender, yellow and pale blue food colourings mixed with clear alcohol (pic 3).

4 Prepare miniature pointed leaves with flower paste/gum paste, using the rose leaf cutter. When dry, hand paint the leaves with

DECORATIVE VARIATION

Miniature cakes such as this two-sided one are especially popular with the New York élite. If there is plenty of preparation time and only a few are required, make the cake in its entirety. If not and the order is for up to 200 cakes, put the back design on the front and leave the back undecorated – a simple, effective and time-saving solution. Make sure the cake is facing out from the table when serving. Each cake will serve two people and can be shared. Place on the table between each couple if this is the case.

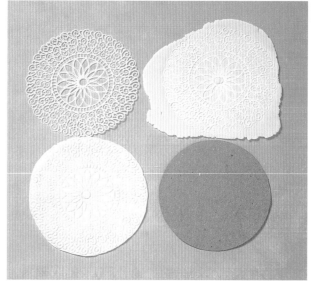

3 *Paint palette indicating centrepiece colours*

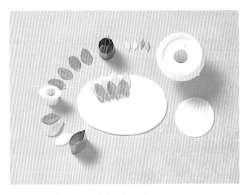

4 Creating the side floral design

moss-green. Attach the leaves to the cake top in two overlapping rings, using edible gum glue. Add the posy mould and fill in the space at the side with tiny lavender, yellow and blue flowers to match the china.

SIDE FLORAL DESIGN

5 Check the centre of the middle tier and mark a circle, using the small centre from the Garrett frill set or the round paper template (see page 153). Beneath this circular decoration, centre and mark the oval floral decoration on the bottom tier (see template on page 153). Prepare pale mint-coloured, ovate leaves in flower paste/gum paste, with the ovate, pointed leaf cutter. Use these to create an outer rim of leaves on the circular and oval marks. For the middle rim, make leaves of the same shape but darker moss-green in colour, and pinch the tips together (pic 4). For the inner rim, attach tiny leaves, made with the miniature rose leaf cutter, coloured with moss-green dust and highlighted with pale lemon dust.

6 Fill the remaining space with miniature roses. For the rose centre, roll up a small strip of flower paste/gum paste, rubbing 2.5 mm/$1/8$ inch from the strip top, till the short end falls off. Cut four paste flowers with the medium blossom cutter. Thin the edges and stack three on top of each other, offsetting the petals each time. Press together in the centre with the veining tool. Cut the last blossom in two, so there are three petals in one unit and two in the other. Wrap the rose centre with two petals, then use edible gum glue to attach the remaining three, offsetting them, into the flower base. Moisten the rose centre base and push into the flower, using the quilting pin. Brush liberally with rubine and cerise dusts (pic 5).

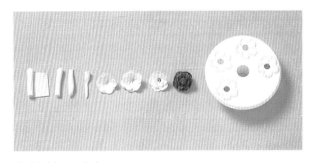

5 Making miniature roses

6 Twisting and colouring the paste strip decoration

FINISHING OFF

7 Cut and run a thin strip of sugarpaste/rolled fondant around the base of each cake. Also prepare two bow loops and tails. Attach these at the base of the top tier, curling the tails on to the cake board. Cover the join with a single rose, miniature blossoms and foliage. The lower tiers look prettier and more delicate with just a single blossom and two miniature rose leaves covering the join. Accent the centre designs with thin rolled scrolls of sugarpaste/rolled fondant or flower paste/gum paste painted with gold highlight powder and clear alcohol/vodka or Everclear.

8 To prevent the cake from slipping on the china, form a thin paste rope and attach with edible gum glue to the inner mouth of the cup. Dry overnight. Place the cake on top of the tea place setting at the reception.

All that Glitters

CAKE AND DECORATION

- 15 cm/6 inch, 20 cm/8 inch and 30 cm/12 inch round cakes
- 6 kg/12 lb white sugarpaste/rolled fondant
- Super gold and super pearl lustre dusts (VB/CK)
- 30 g/1 oz white flower paste/gum paste

EQUIPMENT

- 15 cm/6 inch, 20 cm/8 inch and 30 cm/12 inch thin round cake boards
- Square-patterned embossing tool or similar (see step 1)
- Paper templates for side design (see page 153)
- Fine and medium paintbrushes
- 4 mm and 6 mm beadmaker (CK)
- Medium blossom cutter (RL)
- Dressmaker's tracing wheel
- Quilting pin
- Veining tool
- Lace cutter
- Miniature blossom cutter
- 38 cm/15 inch round cake board
- White ribbon, to trim 38 cm/15 inch round cake board
- 6 x 1 cm/$^1/_2$ inch dowel rods
- 5 x 5mm/$^1/_4$ inch dowel rods
- Long sharpened dowel rod

FOR A LANDMARK WEDDING, WHEN ONLY THE GRANDEST CAKE WILL DO. DRESSED WITH DRAMATIC GOLD SCROLLS, PRECIOUS SUGARED PEARLS AND DAINTY CORONET, THIS IS SURELY A CAKE FIT FOR A QUEEN! WATCH HER FACE GLOW WITH PLEASURE WHEN SHE SEES THIS RICH SCULPTED FANTASY WITH ORNATE BAROQUE DETAIL. DELICIOUS EDIBLE MEMORIES CERTAIN TO PROVOKE COMMENT!

PREPARING THE CAKES

1 Freeze the cakes overnight. Sculpt the top and bottom tiers identically, with a very sharp knife, by paring 1 cm/^{1}/$_2$ inch from the base of each cake graduating up to the top – cut nothing from the top edge. Check to see all sides are even by

1 Embossed paste and tool

spinning on a turntable. For the middle tier, carve from the base upwards and the top downwards, creating a gradual curve and forming a waist 1 cm/^{1}/$_2$ inch deep. Do not remove excessive amounts of cake, because it doesn't take much to alter the silhouette (see page 140). Centre each tier on a matching-sized thin cake board, then cover each cake with sugarpaste/rolled fondant. Immediately emboss a circle of repeat square patterns into the upper edge surface of the top and bottom tiers, using any decorative embossing tool such as a decorative cutlery/flatware handle, button or commercial embossing tool (pic 1).

2 Divide the middle tier into six panels and the bottom tier into twelve. Measure the circumference of the top and bottom cakes with adding machine tape if preferred. Mark the divisions on the tape. Prick each division point with a pin, to act as a guide.

TOP AND BOTTOM TIER SIDE DESIGN

3 Knead, hand roll and mould sugarpaste/rolled fondant scrolls, C-shapes and teardrops. Using the side design templates (see page 153), draw the scroll and C-shapes on a sheet of paper, making sure they fit into the appropriate panels. Use this as a guide to mould each piece so they are a uniform shape. Prepare the teardrops freehand.

4 Paint the moulded pieces using super gold lustre dust mixed with clear alcohol (pic 2). Be careful not to over-paint on to the cake surface or leave fingerprints; over-paint mistakes can be rectified by repainting with pure Everclear and a clean brush. (Everclear does not leave a hole in the paste, nor will there be shiny marks.) Glue the shapes in a repeat pattern on the sides of both cakes (see page 145).

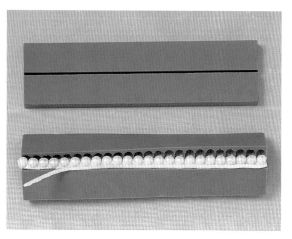

2 Dusting C-shapes and teardrops for the top and bottom tiers

3 Pearl beads in the beadmaker

PEARLS

5 First brush the inside of the beadmaker with super pearl lustre dust. Insert a thick rope of white flower paste/gum paste. Push in firmly and press down over the closure with a rolling pin. Open the mould (pic 3) and tease out the pearls with a palette knife. Cut the bead strips to size. Trim the excess strip with fine scissors.

6 Outline the moulded scrolls and C-shapes on the top tier with 4 mm pearls and on the bottom tier with 6 mm pearls (pic 4), and attach with edible gum glue. Cut out and impress medium blossom flowers into the flower paste/gum paste within the pattern border. Finish off with 16 mm/⅝ inch hand-moulded pearls on the bottom tier.

MIDDLE TIER

7 Measure the depth of the cake. Cut strips of white sugarpaste/rolled fondant 3 cm/1¼ inches wide by the cake depth. Following the line of a ruler, run the dressmaker's tracing wheel down the centre of each. Glue the panels lightly to the cake. (This cake was not measured because it is unimportant how wide the final strip is for the front. The last one is always narrow. If by miscalculation a wider slot appears, split it with an extra row of pearls and add two rows of buttons.) Cover each join with a vertical strip of pearls.

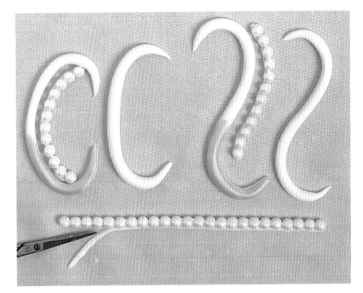

4 Further decorative stages of the scrolls, C-shapes and pearls

5 Painting floral jewellery

CORONET

9 Cut a 18 x 5 cm/7 x 2 inch strip of flower paste/gum paste, then run the lace cutter along one side (pic 6). Allow to firm up for a few minutes. Guide the paste into a small circle using a small tin/can (anything round with a straight edge). Seal the join with a dab of edible gum glue. Attach a thin strip of paste to the base. Paint the edges of the lace with super gold lustre dust mixed with clear alcohol/vodka or Everclear. Carefully attach handmade 2 mm/1/16 inch baby pearls to each of the coronet points, using royal icing. On top of these, add tiny super gold and clear alcohol painted miniature blossoms, each cupping freehand teardrop pearls (pic 7).

FLORAL JEWELLERY

8 For the moment, forget that flower paste/gum paste is always prepared paper thin, and cut out thick paste flowers with the medium blossom cutter. Prick the entire surface with the quilting pin and press in a throat with the veining tool. Paint with super gold lustre dust mixed with clear alcohol/vodka or Everclear (pic 5). Make another strip of pearls and cut them apart with scissors. Attach single pearls to the centre of each 'flower' with gum glue.

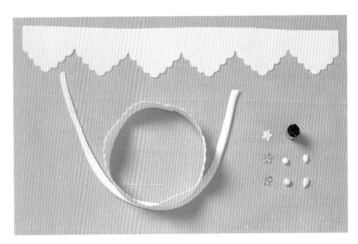

6 Coronet assembly for the cake top

7 Coronet: bird's eye view

EMBELLISHMENT

10 On the centre tier, fit a tiny puffed swag of sugarpaste/rolled fondant between each row of vertical pearls at the top, and cover the join with gold floral jewellery (pic 8).

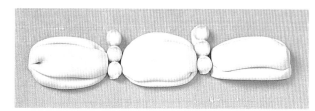

8 Puffed swags with pearl stations

ASSEMBLY

11 Cover the 38 cm/15 inch round cake board with sugarpaste/rolled fondant and band with white ribbon. Edge with 6 mm pearls. Centre the bottom tier on the board.

12 Dowel each tier and stack (see page 142). Sharpen the long dowel and measure alongside the lower two cakes, cut and hammer in centrally. (Normally the dowel would be hammered through all tiers; however, since the top of the cake can be seen through the coronet it would not be visually practical.) Attach the top tier with royal icing. Seal the top and bottom tiers with 6 mm pearl rope borders.

13 Add puffed swags and floral jewellery to the base of the middle tier. Attach gold floral jewellery between the embossed squares on the top cake surface. Glue the coronet on to the top tier, or carry separately to the reception site and then place in position. (Ask the caterers to pack it for the bride once the cake is served.)

SERVING SUGGESTIONS

Before serving, instruct the caterers to remove the heavy scrollwork and beads with a sharp chef's knife. Photocopy the cake cutting chart provided on page 138 and hand to the caterers for a suggested serving procedure.

Marquise de Pompadour

CAKE AND DECORATION

- 15 cm/6 inch, 20 cm/8 inch, 25 cm/10 inch and 30 cm/12 inch oval cakes
- 5 kg/10 lb ivory sugarpaste/rolled fondant
- Aztec-gold, super pearl, oyster and antique silk lustre dusts (VB/CK)
- 15 ml/3 tsp gelatine
- 15 ml/3 tsp Karo syrup or liquid glucose
- 500 g/1 lb ivory flower paste/gum paste

EQUIPMENT

- Piece of costume jewellery or commercial mould if available
- Model magic, latex or silicone
- Kingston cutter former (TOB)
- Medium-sized paintbrush
- Kingston cutters (TOB – medium set)
- 38 cm/15 inch oval cake board
- Ivory ribbon, 1 cm/¹/₂ inch wide, to trim 38 cm/15 inch cake board
- 15 cm/6 inch, 20 cm/8 inch, 25 cm/10 inch and 30 cm/12 inch thin oval cake boards
- Brocade-textured rolling pin (RVO)
- Lace cutter (FMM – M8)
- Dressmaker's tracing wheel
- Satay stick/bamboo skewer
- 19 x 5 mm/¹/₄ inch dowel rods
- Grosgrain-textured rolling pin (EC)
- Sponge foam (optional)
- 3 mm beadmaker (CK)
- Long sharpened dowel rod
- Veining or Dresden tool
- Moulded floral centre cutter (SB – 4662)
- Oval biscuit cutter/cookie cutter (W)

INSPIRED BY THE LAVISH EIGHTEENTH-CENTURY LIFESTYLE OF THE MARQUISE DE POMPADOUR, THIS WEDDING CAKE PAYS TRIBUTE TO SOME OF THE SPECIAL THINGS SHE LOVED: JEWELLERY, BOWS AND ROSETTES. ELEGANT BEYOND BELIEF, THE MARQUISE MADE THE BOW AND ARTIFICIAL FLOWERS HER TRADEMARK; BOTH ARE AS COMPLEMENTARY TO CAKE DESIGN AS THEY ARE TO FASHION.

COSTUME JEWELLERY

1 Create a mould of the chosen piece of costume jewellery, using the model magic, latex or silicone – the last was used in this project (pic 1). Press the sugarpaste/rolled fondant firmly into the mould, then freeze. Remove from the freezer and pop out, right side up, on to a non-stick surface. The paste will sweat a little, but don't touch the surface; just allow it to dry naturally. Trim any excess paste from the edges with a craft knife, scalpel or scissors. Lay on the upper edge of the Kingston former so each piece has a slightly convex shape that conforms to the rose leaf side designs. Dry, then paint with lustre dusts mixed with clear alcohol/vodka or Everclear, using aztec-gold lustre dust for the central 'golden topaz', super pearl lustre dust on the bezel stone surround and oyster lustre dust on the outer 'stones'. Dissolve the gelatine in 30 ml/6 tsp cold water,

1 Handmade sugar costume jewellery

then leave it to sit for 10 minutes until it is spongy, then microwave for a few seconds to liquefy. Add the Karo syrup or liquid glucose, and sit the container in a hot water bath (au bain-marie). Do not cook the mixture, just melt it. Paint the paste jewellery quickly, with the medium-sized brush. Reheat if the mixture begins to thicken and gel.

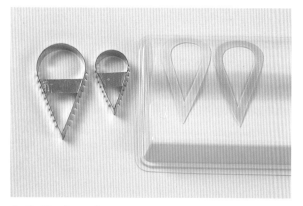

2 Stylized rose leaves, former and cutters

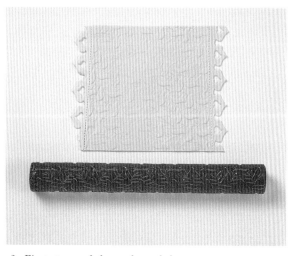

3 First stage of the embossed drapes

2 Roll out the flower paste/gum paste quite thinly and cut the side designs using the Kingston cutters (pic 2). Lay on the Kingston former and dry overnight. For uniformity of curve, make one rose leaf, dry it and rotate it as the first on each former as a guide. Paint with antique silk lustre dust mixed with clear alcohol/vodka or Everclear. Glue the jewelled piece on to the rounded upper end of the rose leaf side design, with royal icing. Set aside until ready to attach to the cake sides.

PREPARING THE CAKES

3 Cover the 38 cm/15 inch cake board with sugarpaste/rolled fondant and set aside to dry overnight. Cover the edge with matching ivory ribbon. Centre and glue each cake on the matching-sized, thin oval cake boards, then cover with paste, bringing it right down over the edge of each board. Centre the bottom tier on the 38 cm/15 inch cake board, securing with a blob of royal icing or a flattened sticky piece of sugarpaste/rolled fondant.

THE DRAPES

4 Prepare four 23 x 23 cm/9 x 9 inch squares of sugarpaste/rolled fondant, using a brocade-textured rolling pin. Thin the edges with a smooth rolling pin. Brush the entire piece with antique silk lustre dust. Embellish the edges with the lace cutter, and run a stitching line with the tracing wheel (pic 3). Brush over the edges with oyster lustre dust. Gather into folds using the satay stick/bamboo skewer (pic 4) and lay carefully on the bottom tier cake. Be alert: the lace pieces can distort

very quickly if you are not paying attention. Pull the corners into a central point at the sides and rest them on the cake board. Flatten the folds where the next tier will sit. Coax the edges into a gentle folded curve with a fluffy paintbrush. Cover the corners with fan-shaped, lace-edged, matching drapes, then highlight with pieces of the paste costume jewellery.

STACKING THE CAKES

5 Insert seven 5 mm/¹/₄ inch dowels into the bottom tier cake (see page 142), following its oval shape. Add the next tier as quickly as possible, because the drapes will crack under the weight of the cake if the sugarpaste/rolled fondant dries too hard. Add a 5 mm/¹/₄ inch band of grosgrain-textured ribbon paste around this third tier cake, using the grosgrain-textured rolling pin. Seal with a small piped bead of ivory royal icing.

4 Second stage of the embossed drape

(Note that the piping on this tier will not be straight because of the flow of the sugar drape.) Attach the jewellery pieces to the rose leaf side designs, with royal icing. As they are top heavy and inclined to slide a little, make sure they aren't slipping before moving on to the next jewellery piece – or support with pieces of foam.

6 Add five 5 mm/¹/₄ inch dowels to the third tier cake, once again following its oval shape. Position the second tier and add the grosgrain-textured ribbons, beads and side designs, as in step 5. Then dowel the second tier cake, centre the top cake on it and decorate the sides, as for the other tiers. Hammer the long sharpened dowel through the centre of the cakes, to stop them slipping (see page 142).

ADVICE TO BEGINNERS
After adding the four top drapes, lightly cover the upper surface of the bottom tier cake with plastic wrap to slow the drying rate. This will give you time to arrange the sides, add the second tier cake, then the fanned corner drape and jewellery.

RUFFLED ROSETTE
7 Cut a 38 x 2.5 cm/15 x 1 inch strip of sugarpaste/rolled fondant or flower paste/gum paste. Trim one side with the lace cutter and frill the edge with the veining or Dresden tool. Gather the edges gently on the unfrilled side, gradually curving into a circle and drawing into the centre (pic 5). Cover the centre with a moulded floral posy. Attach to

the ruffled rosette, then brush the whole piece with antique silk lustre dust, and highlight the edges with oyster lustre dust.

BOWS

8 Prepare the grosgrain-textured bows on the front and rear of the bottom tier by texturing some sugarpaste/rolled fondant, using the grosgrain-textured rolling pin. Cut four pieces 4.5 x 13 cm/1³/₄ x 5 inches, pinch each in at the centre, and attach with royal icing, for the loops. To make the tails, cut eight pieces 4.5 x 18 cm/1³/₄ x 7 inches, pinch each in at one end, and attach. Make sure the royal icing holding the ribbon loops and tails in place is dry before adding the paste jewellery on the bow centre at the front and the ruffled rosette at the back – there is a lot of weight accumulating here.

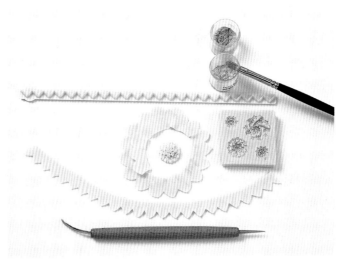

5 Ruffled rosettes and equipment

DOMED JEWELLERY BOX

9 Cut out an ivory flower paste/gum paste base, using the biscuit cutter/cookie cutter. Roll out another piece of paste with the brocade-textured rolling pin. Brush the surface with antique silk lustre dust, then drape over the sharp side of the cutter and leave it for 10–15 minutes (pic 6). Turn it over and cut down hard. Do not touch the dome for an hour or so, until it is set. Measure the circumference of the oval; this will be the length. Cut a 2 cm/³/₄ inch strip by the length measurement, and use it to edge the oval base, cutting neatly at the back and joining all seams with minute dabs of water. When completely dry, add an edging of 3 mm sugar pearls around the domed top and to the box top and base. Brush the beads with antique silk lustre dust.

TRANSPORTING THE CAKE

10 If this cake is too heavy to be carried completely assembled, stack the bottom two tiers and box them. Position the dowels in the next tier and box this and the top tier separately. Temporarily leave off the side designs at both ends of each cake, so there is room for the offset spatulas to be inserted while manoeuvring the cake into position. At the reception, centre the cake into position, pipe the upper borders and add the missing side designs. Wait a few minutes before leaving to be sure the side designs are firmly attached.

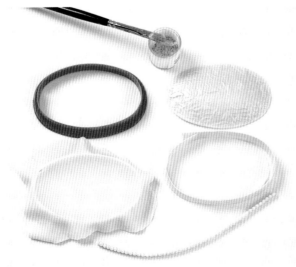

6 Sugar pieces for the domed jewellery box

Tussie Mussie – Vintage Glamour

BOUQUET HOLDER AND DECORATION
- Cream horn former or ice-cream cone
- Cornflour/cornstarch
- 55 g/2 oz white flower paste/gum paste
- Super pearl lustre dust (VB/CK)

EQUIPMENT
- Parchment paper
- Paper template for bouquet holder (see page 154)
- Eyelet cutter (RVO)
- Linen-like fabric, textured rolling pin or lace plastic doily
- Lacy decoration (see step 2)
- Veining tool
- Sponge or cotton wool/cotton balls
- Lace mould (RVO)
- 24-gauge wire
- Rippled foam pieces

The word 'tussie' refers to the bouquet, and 'mussie' to the moss that kept the flowers moist. Tussie mussie holders were mostly made of silver plate and sterling silver, although some were of mother-of-pearl. With the current nostalgia for times past, it seemed appropriate to include this romantic symbol of a bygone era. Indeed, mothers of the bride already commonly carry tussie mussies at prestigious weddings in the United States. This reproduction vintage bouquet holder will hold a petite bouquet that will also make a perfect and unusual cake top.

TUSSIE MUSSIES ARE SMALL POSY HOLDERS AND WERE ORIGINALLY CARRIED BY FORMAL LADIES OF FASHION IN THE VICTORIAN ERA. THESE TINY CONE-SHAPED VASES, FILLED WITH FRAGRANT BOUQUETS, WERE HELD IN THE HAND, MAKING A STROLL IN THE STREET MORE AROMATICALLY PLEASANT.

BASIC TUSSIE MUSSIE CONE

1 Wrap a cream horn former or ice-cream cone with parchment paper and dust with cornflour/cornstarch. Roll out the flower paste/gum paste and cut out the bouquet holder template with a craft knife or scalpel. Decorate the edge of the paste with the

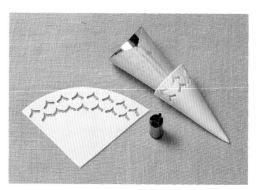

1 Basic paste cone preparation

eyelet cutter, then wrap around the former, overlapping slightly at the back (pic 1). Barely dampen the join with edible gum glue and press firmly together. Brush with super pearl lustre dust, then turn upside down on the former to dry.

2 When the cone is firm enough to handle without collapsing, emboss a strip of flower paste/gum paste with any linen-like fabric or even with a textured rolling pin or lace plastic doily. Fold the embossed paste in half and attach to the inside wall of the cone (pic 2), checking that it is all the same width. Emboss a 5 mm/

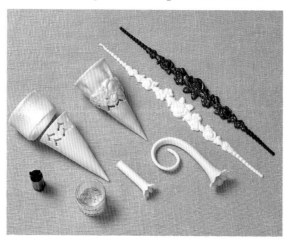

2 Assembly of the decorative stages required

¼ inch strip of flower paste/gum paste on some lacy decoration such as the brass metal strip used here. Cover the rough edge of the join on the paste cone with the embossed paste strip. Brush completely with super pearl lustre dust.

THE HANDLE

3 Prepare a 5 mm/¼ inch log of flower paste/gum paste. Hollow out one end, using the veining tool, then flatten the hollowed-out end and cut eight pointed petals with scissors. Thin them between the thumb and forefinger. Taper the other end to a point and curl round. (If preferred, leave the handle straight, and shorter.) Using the sponge or cotton wool/cotton balls, support the handle until dry. Insert the paste cone into the handle and attach with royal icing; support until dry.

3 Creating the wired lace pieces

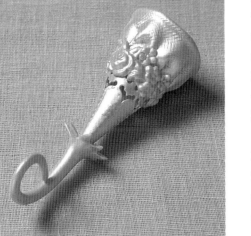

LACE PIECES

4 Brush the lace mould with super pearl lustre dust. Press thinly rolled flower paste/gum paste into the mould, then roll across the cutting surface with a non-stick pin. Remove the lace piece carefully and cut eyelet holes in it with a craft knife or scalpel. Attach to the 24-gauge wire. Dry on the rippled foam, to create unusual shapes (pic 3).

FINISHING OFF

5 Fill the tussie mussie with a flower posy of your choice, such as a pair of tea roses, buds and foliage, as used here, in addition to the wired lace pieces.

Well Dressed in Tulle

PURSE AND DECORATION

- 185 g/6 oz/³/₄ cup sugar
- 30 g/1 oz white flower paste/gum paste (double this if the handle ribbon is also made of paste)
- Red pearl lustre dust (VB/CK)

EQUIPMENT

- 68 cm/27 inches cotton tulle, 23 cm/¹/₄ yard wide (this is more than is needed but the width is necessary)
- Kitchen paper towel
- Large embroidery hoop
- Paper templates for purse (see page 156)
- Piece of stiff plastic or mylar
- Pink ribbon, 2 mm/¹/₁₆ inch wide, to trim the handle (optional)
- Lace mould or embossed material such as lace (see step 5)
- Broderie anglais cutter (PME)
- Plain Lucite stand (optional)

CLASSIC CHIC: THIS PETITE EVENING PURSE MAKES A STUNNING ORNAMENTAL STATEMENT. GLEAMING WITH PEARLIZED VINTAGE FRAMEWORK AND CUSTOMIZED INITIAL, IT OFFERS A NEW TWIST FOR THE UP-TOWN GIRL LOOKING FOR SOMETHING FRESH AND DISTINCTIVE.

PREPARING THE COTTON TULLE

2 Dip and saturate the cotton tulle in the sugar syrup. Drain off the excess and blot lightly. Stretch the tulle in the embroidery hoop (pic 1) and dry completely. Remove the syrup-soaked tulle from the hoop and cut out the purse, using the template.

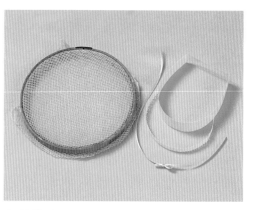

1 Tulle in the hoop, and the handle former

THE HANDLE

3 Cut out a 20 x 1 cm/8 x ¹/₂ inch syrup-soaked tulle strip for the handle. Bend the piece of stiff plastic or mylar into a horseshoe shape and tape in position. Lay the syrup-soaked tulle handle over it, and tape in place, to form an arch. Leave overnight to dry. Cut the material ribbon to size, or make one with flower paste/gum paste, and attach to the handle with edible gum glue. Add a tiny bow of ribbon or paste at the top, before removing the handle from the former.

UGAR SYRUP FOR COTTON TULLE

1 For the sugar syrup, mix the sugar and 125 ml/ 4 fl oz/¹/₂ cup water until it dissolves. Bring to a gentle boil in a small saucepan before reducing to simmer for 10 minutes. Brush down the sides of the pan to incorporate any stray sugar crystals and check that the sugar stays quite clear in colour, with no hint of caramelization. Cool and store in a sealed container in the refrigerator until needed.

2 Folding and shaping the tulle

MAKING THE PURSE

4 On the purse tulle piece, cut two 1 cm/ ¹/₂ inch slits at the centre of each end and running parallel to the sides (pic 2). Set aside. Mark the folds with very faint lines so they won't be seen, then bend the purse piece

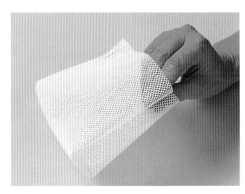

3 Setting the side seams

in half. Press the sides in and push up the triangular tab at the base (pic 3), so it stays in place without stitching. Make one knotted stitch each at the top right and top left, to hold the purse together. Pin the four darts and stitch a single over-sew knot at the top of each dart. Gently encourage the darts to taper off half-way down the front of the purse.

SIDE DECORATION

5 Using the templates (see page 156), prepare an identical pair of moulded top frames and eight triangular edging pieces from the flower paste/gum paste. Brush with red pearl lustre dust. Emboss these paste pieces with the lace mould or any embossed material – mine came from a company specializing in brass furniture mouldings (pic 4). Dry the frames flat. Attach the embossed triangular pieces while damp so that they follow the contour of the tulle, using minute amounts of royal icing. Less is best! Put on the embossed paste frames when dry.

6 Since the 'K' initial is in fact mine, it might be nice to personalize the purse with your own. Draw a pattern of the initial required. Form very thin rolls of flower paste/gum paste, occasionally breaking the lines of the letter by adding broderie anglais paste pieces arranged into flowers. Form the larger, melon-shaped pieces freehand. Brush everything with red pearl lustre dust, then attach with royal icing. Add the handle, slipping the purse top between the vertical slits; secure with royal icing.

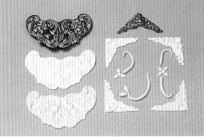

4 Decorative lace frame and corners

OPTIONAL TOUCH
Prepare a simple filler flower bouquet resting on a single leaf, and hook over the edge of the purse framework.

Romantic Foot First

SHOE AND DECORATION

- 75 g/2½ oz flower paste/gum paste
- Peach, antique silk, lime, super gold, copper, super pearl, pink and teal lustre dusts (VB/CK)
- Yellow, lemon, black and buttercup petal dusts (VB/CK)

EQUIPMENT

- Clean aluminium drink can
- Adhesive tape
- Sturdy cardboard
- Paper templates for the shoe (see page 154)
- Plastic wrap
- Textured fabric or embossed rolling pin
- Tiny cutters for eyelet (RVO)
- Curved cardboard
- Tiny rose petal cutter (OP – R4)
- Natural non-toxic leaf
- Tiny filler blossom cutters
- Rose leaf cutter (OP – R5)
- Chrysanthemum cutter (OP – N4)
- Celformers (CC)
- Oak leaf cutters (OP – OL1, OL2, OL3)
- Cotton wool/cotton balls or sponge foam
- Base plaque (OP – P5)

COMPOSING THIS FLORAL GALLERY OF FANTASY FOOTWEAR WAS A DESIGNER INDULGENCE. A MODERN BRIDE LOVES SPECIAL VIGNETTES, SO CREATE A PERSONAL SLIPPER ECHOING THE PATTERN OF HER DRESS, BOUQUET OR TROUSSEAU. THIS WOULD BE A FLATTERING DESIGN CONCEPT!

MAKING THE SHOE

1 Prepare a shoe 'last' from a clean aluminium drink can and tape it vertically on a piece of sturdy cardboard (pic 1). Using the shoe templates (see page 154), cut out the sole and the vamp of the shoe from flower paste/gum paste. Cover the vamp with plastic wrap, then shape the sole over the shoe 'last'.

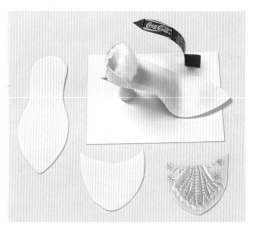

1 Stages of shoe construction

2 Make a freehand paste heel, referring to the templates on page 154. Insert the heel in position and attach with edible gum glue. Imprint the vamp with the textured fabric or embossed rolling pin, then cut eyelet holes (pic 2), using the tiniest cutters available to retain the scale. Attach the vamp to the front of the shoe with edible gum glue

2 Winter White Rose Delight shoe assembly

and push in a piece of curved cardboard to maintain the open shape. Cut out the back of the heel in paste, using the template on page 154, and fix it in position with edible gum glue.

SHOE ASSEMBLY

3 Cover the basic shoe with a selection of paste leaves and flowers. Floral shoes are more entrancing if the leaves are twisted and curved; flowers are generally left alone with little or no distortion. Use the celformers to create different heels by building up leaf combinations, as shown with the oak leaf. Colouring can be matt or pearlized. Normally I work with white or ivory paste and build the colour up as required; however, that does not mean the flower paste/gum paste can't be coloured.

4 Since each shoe is custom designed, cut the leaves in batches of four or five, then colour and add after twisting and curling. It is hard to estimate how many are needed, because each shoe varies. Sometimes the layers can be quite tight, and at other times loose and airy. Be sure to have a sufficient supply of cotton wool/cotton balls or sponge foam, to support the different stages of assembly. Cut out the base plaque, decorate if preferred, then attach the shoe (see also page 69).

SOFT SHADES OF SPRING

Spring finds romance afoot with monochromatic dogwood blossoms and accent foliage. For the dogwood flower, cut out tiny rose petals in flower paste/gum paste, using the rose petal cutter, then brush with a combination of peach and antique silk lustre dusts and attach to a freehand moulded button centre. To vein and shape the dogwood petals, see page 130. Cut leaf slips freehand with a craft knife or scalpel and vein with the natural non-toxic leaf. Brush with peach and antique silk lustre dusts, then twist and curl the paste leaves, before attaching to the back and side of the shoe. Add tiny filler blossoms for extra detail. Form the paste heel, coloured in the same manner as the rest of the shoe, by placing three large rose leaves upside down and drying in the celformer.

SUMMER BLISS SWEET ART'S KISS

Trip into summer with an inlaid embossed vamp, featuring purple and yellow filler blossoms. Take care that the cutters selected are in scale with the shoe. For Vincent Marquetry inlay technique, see page 22. Decorate the vamp with eyelets formed by any combination of very small cutters, making sure the outside edge of the base paste pattern is not distorted. Outline the heel with twisted leafy spears brushed with lime lustre dust and highlighted with super gold lustre dust, then secure with edible gum glue.

Make the tiny button paste chrysanthemums using the chrysanthemum cutter, brush with yellow and lemon petal dusts, and tip the centre with black petal dust. Prepare the leaves for the heel in the same way as for the spring shoe, except they are coloured with lime and super gold lustre dusts.

AUTUMN ESSENTIALS UNCOVERED

Discover nature's ornaments, tiny acorns nestled in satiny copper oak leaves, then pulled together with tiny filler blossoms. Make the acorns freehand, with flower paste/gum paste. Using the graduated set of oak leaf cutters, cut and vein paste leaves and brush on copper lustre dust. Build up the leaves on the shoe back, supporting them with cotton wool/cotton balls. Prepare the heel as for the spring shoe, then dry in the celformer. The only other colours used here were super pearl lustre dust and buttercup petal dust for the accent blossoms.

WINTER WHITE ROSE DELIGHT

Put your best foot forward clad in pretty pink roses and soft teal leaves, made in flower paste/gum paste. The special accents featured on this shoe include a full-blown pink rose heel; winter-white, embossed vamp, and rose foliage forming the outer silhouette. For the pink rose, the petals must be damp when centring the heel. Build up the back of the heel, then add a miniature rose bud for accent. Brush this shoe with super pearl, teal and pink lustre dusts. (To make the roses, see page 94.)

FLORAL SHOES

Making floral shoes can be tricky and requires patience. The method outlined on pages 66–7 is for a basic shoe, which can be decorated in any manner required. Each shoe is about 13 cm/ 5 inches from toe to heel and, for display purposes, is on a base plaque. It can, however, be attached directly to the cake top. Most brides prefer to keep their shoe as a permanent souvenir, and a plaque does help to inhibit breakage as the shoe is not handled.

Petite Gilded Cottage

COTTAGE AND DECORATION

- 500 g/1 lb white flower paste/gum paste
- Super gold and super pearl lustre dusts (VB/CK)
- 30 g/1 oz/2 tbsp caster/superfine sugar

EQUIPMENT

- Thin cardboard templates for the gilded cottage (see pages 154–5)
- Square broderie anglais cutter (PME)
- Veining tool
- Sponge foam
- Ball tool
- Paintbrush
- Small plastic bridal umbrella, with handle removed

THE STAR OF ITS OWN SHOW, THIS TINY TREASURE COULD STEAL YOUR HEART AWAY. THE FAÇADE SHIMMERS UNDER A GENTLE MANTLE OF POWDERED SUGAR SNOW. A SPECIAL CONFECTION DEDICATED TO LORD WEDGWOOD, WHO HAS ENCOURAGED MY SUGARCRAFT ENDEAVOURS FOR MANY YEARS.

THE WALLS

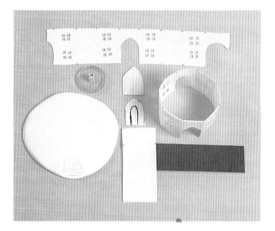

1 Basic walls and cottage base

1 Prepare a paper template of the cottage (see pages 154–5), marking the fold lines of the walls and cutting out slightly enlarged window and door positions. Roll the flower paste/gum paste into an oblong. Lay the paper template on top of the paste and cut around the perimeter of the walls, with a sharp craft knife or scalpel, being careful not to drag the paste; continually wipe the knife with a damp cloth if the paste seems to resist. Cut out the windows with the square broderie anglais cutter, then the front door and rear arch with the knife. Discard the window pieces but retain the door shape. Mark in the door mouldings and the knob; brush with super gold lustre dust, and paste on to a slightly larger piece of paste similar in shape (pic 1). Using the veining tool, press into the paste to form the frame around the front doorway, taking care not to distort the shape. Lightly brush the door frame and door with super gold lustre dust.

2 Bend the straight-edged piece of cardboard at the fold lines for the walls. Lay the paste walls on top of this cardboard template, to ensure the lines are straight, and gently adjust it to follow the bends in the cardboard. Stand the paste walls upright against the base of the cardboard template. Join the walls at the back arch using edible gum glue. Remove the cardboard, add the front door from the inside, and fill the interior with sponge foam, for support. Leave the wall structure until absolutely dry.

THE BASE

3 Mould a slightly elevated flower paste/gum paste mound and shape it to fit into the base template (see page 155). Make the central area, where the structure will sit, perfectly flat. Press in the steps with the veining tool, and roll the ball tool along the edge, to form a little bank. Set aside to dry. Move the wall structure into position and attach with royal icing. Using a paintbrush, lightly dampen the base with water and sprinkle with caster/superfine sugar to create a snow blanket effect.

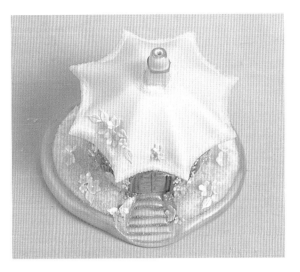

THE ROOF

4 Using the template (see page 155), cut the ceiling support from flower paste/gum paste and dry thoroughly. Using the plastic bridal umbrella as a base former, prepare paste spokes and arrange them in eight even separations (pic 2). Allow to dry. Cut an extremely thin sheet of paste for the overhanging roof (see template on page 154) with its diameter 1 cm/1/2 inch larger than that of the ceiling support, and dry.

5 Make a central post of flower paste/gum paste to support the spokes and centre on the ceiling support piece. Assembling the roof will be a fragile exercise, so do take care. Very gently remove the spokes from the former and centre on the ceiling support (pic 3). Gingerly drape the extremely thin overhanging roof paste over the spokes, bringing it right over the edges of the ceiling support. Smooth between the spokes, running the finger tips up and down and forming soft channels. Using a slightly dampened, very sharp craft knife or scalpel, cut the excess away, following the base shape. Insert minute edible gum glue spots under the edge, to hold the roof in place. When thoroughly dry, attach the cottage roof to the walls with royal icing. Paint a 5 mm/1/4 inch stripe with a water-dampened brush around the edge of the roof and dust with caster/superfine sugar, to suggest snow.

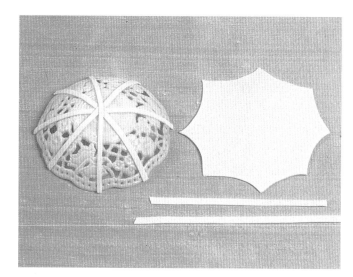

2 First stage of the ceiling support and spokes

3 Second stage of the ceiling support and spokes

THE CHIMNEY

6 Using the chimney template (see page 155), mould the chimney with flower paste/gum paste, and attach to the cottage roof with royal icing. Paint thin horizontal rings around it, using a soupy mixture of super gold lustre dust and clear alcohol/vodka or Everclear.

FINISHING OFF

7 Decorate the walls with miniature white flowers and foliage brushed with super pearl lustre dust. Add accent brush stroke flourishes with super gold lustre dust mixed with clear alcohol/vodka or Everclear before outlining the window treatments and archway.

Spring Basket Show Stopper

BASKET AND DECORATION

- 30 g/1 oz mauve flower paste/gum paste
- 15 g/½ oz white flower paste/gum paste
- Mustard-yellow food colouring (VB/CK)
- Buttercup petal dust (VB/CK)
- 250 g/8 oz/1 cup caster/superfine sugar
- 55 g/2 oz ivory flower paste/gum paste
- Antique silk lustre dust (VB/CK)
- 15 woodland violets (see page 118)
- 4 white tea roses (see page 94)

EQUIPMENT

- Veining or Dresden tool
- Purple stamens
- Green floral tape
- 26-gauge wire
- Set of mini jonquil cutters (Angela Priddy) or a mini chrysanthemum cutter and a small blossom cutter
- Throat tool
- Original vase or oval-shaped container to be duplicated
- Melon baller or spoon
- Fine-grain sandpaper or emery board
- Parsley cutter or sharp knife
- Dressmaker's tracing wheel
- Petal pad
- Sturdy, plastic handle former
- Daisy centre mould (J)
- Small polystyrene/styrofoam block, to fit inside basket

BE-RIBBONNED MOULDED SUGAR BASKET CONTAINS A SPRING CONCOCTION OF IVORY TEA ROSES FLECKED WITH TOUCHES OF MAUVE, PAPER WHITE JONQUILS AND WOODLAND VIOLETS. HONOURS THE FRENCH HOUSE OF LESAGE, MAKERS OF EXQUISITE LACES AND EMBROIDERY.

LILAC BLOSSOMS

1 Form a small cone of mauve flower paste/gum paste, then cut into four equal sections using a pair of fine scissors. Holding the paste flower between the thumb and forefinger, roll each of the stubby petals back and forth with the veining or Dresden tool until quite thin. Trim the petals into a point, then soften them with the finger tips before scoring the top surface with the tip of the scissors (pic 1). Hollow the centre with the thin point of the veining or Dresden tool. Thread a purple stamen through the centre. Attach with floral tape to short lengths of 26-gauge wire and tape into small bunches.

1 Lilac blossom assembly and equipment

2 Paper white jonquil in progress

PAPER WHITE JONQUILS

2 Prepare a small cone of white flower paste/gum paste, then flatten into a Mexican hat. Press the larger jonquil cutter down over the cone and pull away the excess paste. Then cut out the smaller jonquil blossom (pic 2). Thin the petals and centre the smaller trumpet over the larger.

Bond them together at the centre with the throat tool. Paint the calyx on with a little mustard-yellow food colouring mixed with clear alcohol/vodka or Everclear. Brush a tiny spot of buttercup petal dust in the centre. Floral tape the stems.

MAKING THE MOULDED SUGAR BASKET

3 Mix the caster/superfine sugar with 10 ml/2 tsp water – the texture should be like damp sea sand. Firmly pack the dampened sugar into the vase or oval-shaped container to be duplicated (pic 3), then up-end on to a flat dry surface such as dry cardboard, just like making a sandcastle. Transfer to an oven set at 95°C/200°F/GM1/4, and dry for about 15 minutes.

This will create a 5 mm/1/4 inch hard shell on the outside. Hollow out the centre by gently removing the soft sugar with the melon baller or spoon (pic 4), taking care to follow the contour of the mould. Use a fine-grain sandpaper or emery board to neaten any rough edges. If the moulded piece breaks, just crush the sugar back into its original damp sea-sand state, and remould. Turn off the oven and put the moulded piece back in it, to dry thoroughly.

BASKET SIDE DESIGN

4 Brush thinly rolled ivory flower paste/gum paste with antique silk lustre dust and run the parsley cutter or sharp

3 Packing down the dampened sugar

knife across it, forming ribbons. Decorate the ribbon edges
with the tracing wheel, and glue to the moulded basket (pic 5).

4 Hollowing out the sugar mould

BASKET HANDLE

5 Using the petal pad, roll one or two thin ropes of ivory flower paste/gum paste to uniform thickness, depending if a
plain or twisted handle is required. For the latter, twist the ropes together as tightly as possible, without stretching or
breaking them. Brush with antique silk lustre dust. Insert a sturdy plastic handle former inside the moulded basket.
Drape the twisted ropes over the plastic former and allow to dry thoroughly. Cover the joins at the sides with decorative
paste buttons made with the daisy centre mould.

5 Side design and handle attachment

SUGAR MOULDING

This simple method of sugar moulding is taken
to new heights by adding elegant finishing
touches. It is an interesting way to create shapes
suitable for applying all types of decorative side
design. Lots of basic shapes can be made using
all sorts of readily available household items
from yoghurt cups to crystal vases. Pieces can
be combined to create unique containers: for
example, a saucer shape atop a candleholder
base makes a very nice pedestal compote.

FINISHING

6 Make a large soft embossed bow from ivory flower paste/gum paste. Brush
with antique silk lustre dust and attach to the side of the moulded basket.
Insert the polystyrene/styrofoam block in the moulded basket and secure with
edible gum glue. Fill with flowers of your choice. Prepare the lilac and paper
white jonquils as described here. For the woodland violets and tea roses, see
pages 118 and 94. Touches of violet in any flower arrangement add striking
contrast, which in turn accents the dominant flower.

Strings Play the Heart

VIOLIN AND DECORATION

- 55 g/2 oz white flower paste/gum paste
- Super pearl lustre dust (VB/CK)
- 10 paper white jonquils (see page 73)

EQUIPMENT

- Paper templates for the violin (see page 155)
- Palette knife
- Cocktail stick/toothpick
- Cotton wool/cotton ball
- Tiny five-petal flower cutters
- Tiny rose leaf cutter
- Paper white cutter

> *Before beginning this project, take a look at a picture of a real violin*

FOR CENTURIES THE VIOLIN HAS CAPTURED THE ESSENCE OF ROMANCE. PERHAPS THIS DAINTY FLORAL INTERPRETATION IS AN APPEALING ALTERNATIVE TO THE TRADITIONAL SPRAY. TO CONVEY A ROMANTIC THEME, SURROUND IT WITH A COLLAGE OF SUGAR FLOWERS, RIBBONS AND MUSICAL NOTES.

THE BODY

1 Roll out the flower paste/gum paste fairly thinly and, following the template, cut out the top and the bottom of the instrument body. Using a very sharp craft knife, scalpel or other suitable cutter, incise a pair of thin scrolls on the upper surface of the violin body. This will be the top of the instrument. Allow both sides to dry, then brush with super pearl lustre dust.

2 Measure the exterior perimeter of the instrument casing, then cut a 1 cm/^{1}/$_2$ inch wide strip of flower paste/gum paste of the same length plus a little surplus, to be on the safe side. Let the paste set for a few minutes. Paint a very thin strip of edible gum glue just a fraction inside the perimeter of the instrument bottom. Following the contour of the body, stand the strip up on the glue line, like a little dam (pic 1). Don't fight the paste – it will respond to gentle guidance. Trim to fit, then allow to dry before adding the instrument top and attaching with edible gum glue. Fill any discrepancy where the joins meet with royal icing, adding it from the inside. Carefully trowel away any residue with the palette knife.

THE NECK

3 Form the neck of the violin freehand, checking against the template that it is the correct size. Puncture two holes on either side with a cocktail stick/toothpick and push in string pins made from paste. Roll and curl the neck end to form a graceful scroll. While soft and malleable, attach the neck to the casing with edible gum glue, then prop to dry for twenty-four hours. Glue the fret in place.

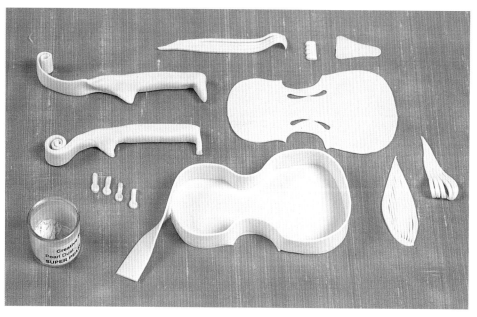

1 *Components for creating the violin*

STRINGS AND DECORATION

4 For the strings and other ornamentation, cut strips of flower paste/gum paste and incise without separating them. Allow them to dry slightly before twisting under and guiding into an easy scroll. Don't be in a hurry. Prop them with a puff of cotton wool/cotton ball, if necessary.

5 To decorate the violin, cut out any miniature filler flowers – they can be any basic five-petalled flower – and rose leaf foliage. Use the paper white cutter to make the ten large paper white jonquils in flower paste/gum paste (see page 73).

Fabulous Faux Fabergé Eggs

Egg and Decoration

- 1 kg/2 lb white chocolate (summer coat)
- Classic ivory, seafoam and peach-coloured white chocolate (summer coat) pastilles (or substitute with oil-based colours specifically for chocolate)
- 55 g/2 oz white flower paste/gum paste
- 55 g/2 oz seafoam flower paste/gum paste
- 55 g/2 oz peach flower paste/gum paste
- Super pearl and avocado-green lustre dusts (VB/CK)
- Cornflour/cornstarch

Equipment

- VIP Whistler or double boiler
- 18 cm/7 inch egg mould (CK)
- Paintbrush
- Fine cotton gloves (optional)
- Egg stand mould (CK)
- Cocktail stick/toothpick
- Rose leaf cutters (OP – R6 and R6a)
- Rose petal cutter (OP – R3)
- Lace-embossed moulds (SB)
- Small filler blossom cutters (PME – plunger small and medium; or OP – F2M and F2L)
- 4 mm beadmaker (CK)
- Berling reproduction mould (ADM – SLL 100)
- Thin kitchen rolling pin
- 5 cm/2 inch egg mould (CK)
- Carnation cutter (OP – C2)
- Ball tool
- Maple leaf cutters (RL)

EXCLUSIVE CONFECTIONS, IMPOSSIBLY DELICIOUS, IMPERIAL HIGH STYLE. CUSTOM-DESIGNED, ELEGANT EGGS MAKE ULTIMATE WEDDING FAVOURS. THOSE WHO SHARE THE LOVE OF FINE TASTE AND THE CONFECTIONER'S ART WILL UNDOUBTEDLY TREASURE THESE BEAUTIFUL EGGS.

MAKING THE EGG

1 Pour water into the spout of the VIP Whistler and replace the whistle. Heat until warm to the hand. The temperature will be maintained for 20 minutes. Gently re-warm as necessary. If using a double boiler, heat the water until hand hot, then proceed. Add the white

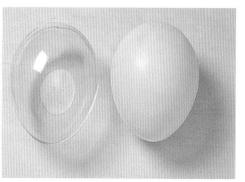

1 Basic ivory egg and mould

chocolate and allow to melt (see page 134). Transfer 250 g/8 oz at a time to a clean mixing bowl and add a coloured white chocolate pastille, to create the required colour. Make one 18 cm/7 inch egg in each colour: classic ivory, seafoam and peach.

2 Pour the coating into the egg mould and swish up the sides with a paintbrush. Refrigerate for a few minutes and paint the sides again from the pooled chocolate in the base. This will strengthen the sides. Return to the refrigerator for 10 minutes, until the chocolate begins to separate from the mould. Remove from the mould; if the chocolate egg is a little stubborn, just tap the mould open side down on the work surface/countertop and it will pop right out when it is ready. If you force the egg out, ugly dull patches will appear. Wearing fine cotton gloves to protect the egg surface, touch the edges of each matching pair of egg halves to the surface of a warm, non-stick frying pan and self-glue together. Very quickly, check from all sides to be sure they are even (pic 1).

EGG DECORATION

3 Cover each basic egg with a selection of decorative pieces, attaching them with tiny dabs of melted chocolate.

Classic czarina (left); Empress Catherine (back); Princess peach (right)

CLASSIC CZARINA

1 Prepare the classic ivory-coloured white chocolate egg. For the stand, pour some ivory-coloured, white chocolate into the egg stand mould (pic 2). Allow to set, then remove and attach to the base of the egg.

2 Prepare the seven stephanotis flowers by forming some white flower paste/gum paste into a Mexican hat (pic 3). Hollow out the centre with the cocktail stick/toothpick and divide equally into five petals. Snip, shape to a point with scissors, and pinch the petals. Dust with super pearl lustre dust.

2 Classic ivory egg stand and mould

3 Stages of the stephanotis flowers

3 For the five rose leaves, cut some white flower paste/gum paste with the rose leaf cutter (R6). Vein, shape and allow to dry. Dust with super pearl lustre dust. Make the three roses by cutting white paste petals with the rose petal cutter. Prepare the centre cone and allow to dry. Add two petals, then three, and then sets of five, offsetting each row from the last. Twist the petals so they look life-like (pic 4). Prepare three rose buds. Set aside to dry. Brush over all with super pearl lustre dust.

4 Prepare the two lace-embossed pieces. Press thinly rolled, white flower paste/gum paste into the lace moulds, remove and trim the edges if necessary. Brush with super pearl lustre dust. Cut two slits at the centre and open out (pic 5). Lay on the top of the egg immediately, attaching with melted chocolate.

4 Rose, leaves and cutter

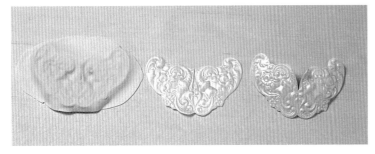

5 Lace-embossed pieces in three stages

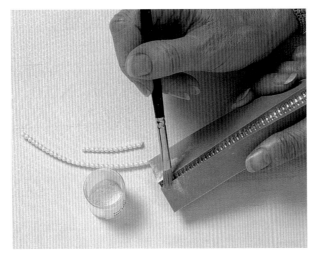

6 Brushing the pearl beads with lustre dust

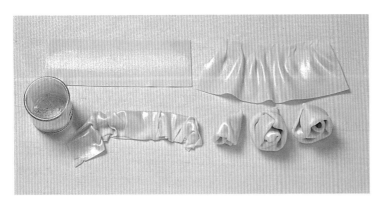

7 Making fabric-effect roses

5 Make the filler flowers, using the small blossom cutters, and follow in a gentle arc at the front of the egg, outlining the lace-embossed pieces. Prepare the pearls in the beadmaker, then brush with super pearl lustre dust (pic 6). Attach a strip of pearls within the arc, at the centre and base. Make the filigree paste shape. Build up the pattern with the roses, buds and stephanotis, then the filigree shape and rose leaves.

EMPRESS CATHERINE

1 Prepare the seafoam-coloured white chocolate egg. For the twelve fabric-effect roses, roll out 15 x 4 cm/6 x 1¹/₂ inch strips of seafoam flower paste/gum paste. Brush only the centre with super pearl lustre dust. Gather one side, then fold in half lengthways. Turn one corner down, then loosely roll up (pic 7). To make the six fabric-effect leaves, cut another paste strip of the same size and brush only the centre strip with super pearl lustre dust. Fold in half, then fold both tails down, to create a triangular point. Pinch the ends together and trim (pic 8).

2 For the twelve latticework leaves, roll out some seafoam flower paste/gum paste. Dust the Berling reproduction mould lightly with cornflour/cornstarch, then press in the paste. Trim the paste, then razor across the top of the mould with a sharp knife.

Remove carefully. Immediately attach six of these latticework leaves in a flower pattern on top of the seafoam egg. Leave the remaining six leaves draped over a thin kitchen rolling pin, to allow them to dry in shape (pic 9). Then attach the latticework leaves and fabric-effect roses and leaves.

PRINCESS PEACH

1 Prepare the peach-coloured white chocolate egg. Make the solid 5 cm/ 2 inch egg in peach-coloured white chocolate. To make each of the eight carnations (pic 10), you should cut four peach-coloured flower paste/gum

8 Preparing the fabric-effect leaves

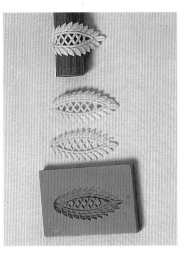

9 Latticework leaves and mould

paste pieces, using the carnation cutter. Frill the edges of all four of them and place three pieces on top of each other. Press the centre gently with the ball tool, forcing the sides upward. Fold the fourth piece into an S-shape and insert it in the centre.

2 Measure and divide the large egg into eight equal parts. Prepare and attach eight peach flower paste/gum paste swags with melted chocolate. Prepare and attach eight tightly controlled drapes, to cover the joins.

3 Cut seventeen maple leaves from white flower paste/gum paste with the maple leaf cutter. Vein, shape and colour them with avocado-green lustre dust. Also in white paste, make a pair of thin bow loops and three twisted tails, and brush with super pearl lustre dust. Glue the 5 cm/2 inch egg on top of the large egg with melted chocolate, add the maple leaves, then the carnations, bow loops and twist tails.

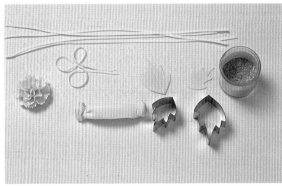

10 Stages of the carnations and maple leaves

Pretty Petals – Precious Pastels

CAKE AND DECORATION

- 2 x 18 cm/7 inch firm-textured, round cakes, 8 cm/3 inches deep, such as chocolate mud or madeira/pound cakes
- 15 cm/6 inch round cake, 2.5 cm/1 inch deep
- 175 g/6 oz ivory flower paste/gum paste
- Ruby and antique silk lustre dusts (VB/CK)
- 1.5 kg/3 lb champagne-coloured sugarpaste/rolled fondant
- Salmon-pink and white liquid or powdered food colourings

EQUIPMENT

- 18-gauge wire
- Medium and large rose petal cutters (OP – R2 and R1)
- Stripes and spots stencils (CSD)
- Plastic lace doily
- Small make-up sponge
- Celformer (CC)
- Drying rack
- Medium blossom plunger cutter (PME)
- Cream floral tape
- Medium and large rose leaf cutters
- 25 cm/10 inch round cake board
- Spray bottle
- Corrugated cardboard (recycle the white liner from biscuit or cookie packets)
- 2 x 18 cm/7 inch thin round cake boards
- 5 x 5 mm/^{1}/$_4$ inch dowel rods
- Small fan brush
- 3 mm beadmaker (CK)
- Tassel stencils (CSD or Delta)
- Dressmaker's tracing wheel
- Veining or Dresden tool
- Celpick (CC)

A NEW TAKE ON THE CAMELLIA. THIS IS AN UPDATED CONTEMPORARY CAKE APPEALING TO THOSE WITH A MORE WHIMSICAL SENSE OF STYLE. FANTASY TAKES FLIGHT AS EACH WHORL OF PETALS IS EITHER STRIPED OR SPOTTED, THEN FABRIC EMBOSSED. NOTE THE EXUBERANT PAINTED SIDE DESIGN, ALL HAND APPLIED IN WARM SHADES OF ROSE AND GOLD WITH GENTLE WAVES OF SMUDGED IVORY PEEPING THROUGH.

CAMELLIA FLOWERS

1 Form the flower centre freehand with ivory flower paste/gum paste and attach to a hooked 18-gauge wire; then dry overnight. For the innermost layer of petals, cut five medium rose petals in paste and thin the edges. Stencil the striped pattern with ruby lustre dust. Lay the petals face down on the plastic lace doily; do not move them about or they will smudge. Emboss the petals on the doily by pressing on the back of each petal with a small make-up sponge; take great care not to distort the coloured stripes. Attach them around the flower centre, overlapping each petal, before slipping the final petal beneath the first, so the effect is continuous.

2 Clean the board surface and stencils (both front and back) with a piece of foam sponge each time they are used, to avoid ghost images and smudging. It is too time-consuming to wash the stencil each time, so roll the flower paste/gum paste on a separate board to the one on which colour is used.

3 Prepare five petals for the second layer, again using the medium rose petal cutter, stencilling with stripes and embossing. Shape each petal in the celformer, curling the top of the petal back over

1 Building up layers of petals

the top. As soon as the petals begin to hold their shape, attach with edible gum glue to the flower and hang upside down on a drying rack.

4 Prepare the third and fourth layers as in step 3, except that the large rose petal cutter is used and the third layer is stencilled with spots (pic 1). Hang upside down to dry completely. Make the paste 'calyx', using the medium blossom plunger cutter, and attach beneath the flower. Steam lightly about 30 cm/12 inches from the boiling water source. Dry without touching. Floral tape the wires in cream.

ROSE LEAVES

5 Cut the leaves from flower paste/gum paste, using the medium and large rose leaf cutters. Stencil the spots and stripes and emboss on the lace doily (pic 2). Allow to dry on a slightly uneven surface, to suggest movement.

PREPARING THE CAKE

6 Cover the 25 cm/10 inch round cake board with sugarpaste/rolled fondant, and dry overnight. Mist with water from the spray bottle, and sponge with a combination of salmon-pink

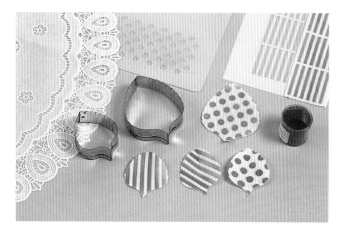

2 Fantasy foliage

and white food colouring. While the surface is still wet, use the piece of corrugated cardboard to create fanciful patterns (pic 3). After the design has dried, brush with antique silk lustre dust.

7 Centre each 18 cm/7 inch cake on a similarly sized, trimmed thin cake board. Stack them both and provide dowel support (see page 142). Cover with sugarpaste/rolled fondant and allow to firm overnight, then add a 15 cm/6 inch, paste-covered cake on top. Centre on the cake board and attach with royal icing. Masking the cake board with greaseproof/wax paper, mist with water and sponge with a combination of salmon-pink and white food colouring. When dry, highlight the surface with broad, fan-brush strokes of ruby lustre dust mixed with clear alcohol/vodka or Everclear, then soften with antique silk lustre dust.

3 Cake colouring and painting steps

RIBBONS AND PEARLS

8 Add a strip of stencilled sugarpaste/rolled fondant around the base of the cake, then another strip folded in half around the top cake. Band the folded strip with a row of 3 mm pearls, made with the beadmaker and coloured with ruby lustre dust. Prepare a wide strip of stencilled paste, then fold the edges under and drape around the board, adding stencilled knots at even intervals.

THE TASSELS

9 Make two paste tassels with the appropriate stencils, pushing them well into the stencil so they are thick and have good definition. Colour with ruby lustre dust before removing from the stencil (pic 4), then 'stitch' along the edge with the tracing wheel before shredding the ends of the tassels with a craft knife or scalpel. Finally thin the edges with the veining or Dresden tool and attach offset to the left side of the cake. Dry and glue into position on the cake board. Add a camellia corsage at the centre. Press the celpick deep into the centre of the cake, then arrange the camellias. Slip the foliage beneath the flower arrangement and secure with edible gum glue.

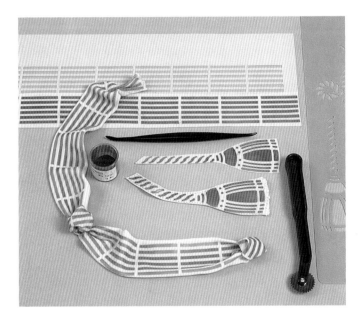

4 Creating the ribbons and tassels

Reception Confection

CAKE AND DECORATION

- 15 cm/6 inch and 20 cm/8 inch round cakes
- 2 kg/4 lb soft lavender-blue sugarpaste/ rolled fondant
- Super gold, antique silk, golden bronze and avocado-green lustre dusts (VB/CK)
- 125 g/4 oz milk chocolate-coloured flower paste/gum paste
- 15 g/$^{1}/_{2}$ oz mid-green flower paste/ gum paste
- 85 g/3 oz soft lavender-blue flower paste/ gum paste
- Two-toned roses and buds (see page 106)
- Cake separator mould (see step 7)

EQUIPMENT

- 15 cm/6 inch and 20 cm/8 inch thin round cake boards
- Small double-edged scalloped crimper (PME)
- Large and small stylized leaf cutters (RVO) or paper templates (see page 157)
- Fine quilting pin
- Dressmaker's tracing wheel
- Ribbon insertion tool (J)
- Plastic lace cake stand (W)
- 14 cm/5½ inch cake plate
- 38 cm/15 inch round cake board
- Soft lavender-blue ribbon, 1.5 cm/⅝ in wide
- Grosgrain-textured rolling pin (EC)
- Double-sided lace mould (ELI – 305)
- Arch cutter (FMM – 1)
- Tiny leaf cutter (RVO)
- Primrose cutters (OP – F3S and F3M)
- Throat tool
- Round piping tube/tip (W – 2)
- Tiny five-petal blossom cutter (RVO)
- Drying rack

A GENTLE WASH OF SOFT LAVENDER-BLUE SUGAR BISQUE ACCENTED WITH SHIMMERING, SOFT, MILK CHOCOLATE-COLOURED GROSGRAIN RIBBONS. FANTASY PRIMROSES AND NEW-LOOK CLASSIC ROSES DECORATE A SUMMER WEDDING CAKE TO TOUCH YOUR HEART. THE SIMPLE CAKE STAND MASQUERADES AS A TIERED CAKE, ADDING EXTRA HEIGHT AND THE ILLUSION OF SIZE.

SCULPTING THE CAKES

1 Freeze the cakes overnight. Starting at the top, pare away thin uniform layers until the cakes appear evenly graduated (see page 140). Be sure to take the height of the cake separator into consideration. Remove a 2.5 cm/1 inch diameter centre from the matching-sized, thin round cake boards, then centre the cakes on them.

PREPARING THE CAKES

2 Cover each cake with soft lavender-blue sugarpaste/rolled fondant, bringing the paste over the edge of the thin round cake boards. Decorate the upper surface of the top tier with the scalloped crimper. Remove a 2.5 cm/1 inch core from the centre of the bottom cake. Hollow out a small amount from the base of the top tier to accommodate the capping bolt on the post.

3 Divide the cake into four. Using the paper templates (see page 157) and quilting pin, prick the flower placement design on the sides of the cakes. Imprint a sunray pattern of branch lines with the tracing wheel. Paint along these lines with super gold lustre dust mixed with clear alcohol/vodka or Everclear. Cut slits into the upper surface and into the cake sides between the repeat floral design, using the insertion tool and following the curve of the ribbon template (see page 157).

1 Stages of the stylized leaves

STYLIZED LEAVES

4 Roll out milk chocolate-coloured flower paste/gum paste and cut out the leaves using the stylized leaf cutters or paper templates (see page 157) – the small cutter is for the top tier and the larger one for the bottom. Brush with antique silk lustre dust and highlight with golden bronze and avocado-green lustre dusts (pic 1).

CAKE STAND

5 Remove the centre column from the plastic lace cake stand. Cover the stand top and base with soft lavender-blue sugarpaste/rolled fondant. Layer the column with paste stylized leaves, securing them in position with edible gum glue. Reassemble the stand and dry overnight.

CAKE BOARD

6 Cover the 38 cm/15 inch round cake board with soft lavender-blue sugarpaste/rolled fondant. Glue the decorated cake stand in the centre with royal icing. Dress the base edge of the cake stand with additional paste leaves. Trim the board with ribbon.

MOULDED SUGAR VASE

7 Prepare a moulded sugar vase (see pages 74–5), using a simple container matching the visible height

of the centre post – this one was recycled from a takeaway meal. Hollow out the centre to match the 2.5 cm/1 inch diameter of the centre post.

RIBBON STRIPS

8 Roll out and emboss milk chocolate-coloured flower paste/gum paste with the grosgrain-textured rolling pin. Cut in strips, using a parsley cutter, craft knife or scalpel. Run along both edges with the tracing wheel. Brush with antique silk lustre dust. Set the ribbon strips aside until needed, by covering with plastic wrap, then placing a damp towel on top. They will be usable for a day kept in this manner.

3 Miniature leaves and blossoms

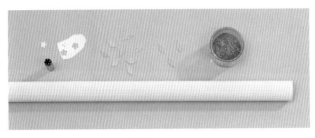

4 Making primroses for the side details

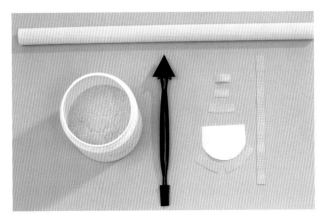

5 Stages of the ribbon insertion

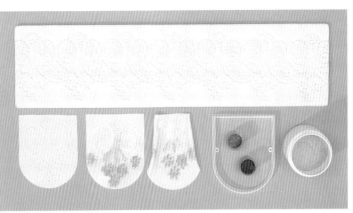

2 Decorative panels for the cake stand

DECORATIVE PANELS

9 Roll out soft lavender-blue sugarpaste/rolled fondant into a strip, then press into the lace mould. Cut out eleven lace-embossed panels using the arch cutter. Brush with antique silk lustre dust, then colour the lace-embossed flowers and leaves with golden bronze and avocado-green lustre dusts (pic 2). Fold the sides under and attach each panel over the edge of the cake board, yet far enough into the centre so that when the cakes are positioned they will cover each panel top.

DECORATING THE CAKES

10 Gum glue the stylized leaves to the cake sides. Emboss mid-green flower paste/gum paste, using the grosgrain-textured rolling pin. Form tiny leaves with the leaf cutter (pic 3) and attach to the cake sides along the golden branch lines.

PRIMROSES

11 Cut out soft lavender-blue flower paste/gum paste primroses, using the primrose cutters (pic 4). Thin the edges and press straight into the side of the cake with the throat tool. Using the round piping tube/tip, add a tiny bead of royal icing to each flower centre. Add extra definition along the branch lines by cutting out and pressing in tiny, blue, five-lobed blossoms.

RIBBON INSERTION

12 Using the ribbon strips that have already been prepared, cut and shape small curved pieces (pic 5) for the ribbon insertion. Using the insertion tool, press curved ribbon strips into slits on the upper surface and cake sides, between the repeat floral design.

RIBBON LOOPS

13 Cut more embossed-paste strips into pieces 9 cm/3¹/₂ inches long, then double them over to form ribbon loops. Pinch the ends together, then hang on a drying rack to retain shape (pic 6).

CAKE TOP CENTREPIECE

14 Pipe a little royal icing in the centre of the top tier. Arrange the ribbon loops in a circle with the ends in the piped royal icing. Begin to layer them and in between tuck two-toned roses and buds (pic 7; although the unusual colour combination and the alternate petal placement are just for this project). Support in position with sponge foam until quite dry.

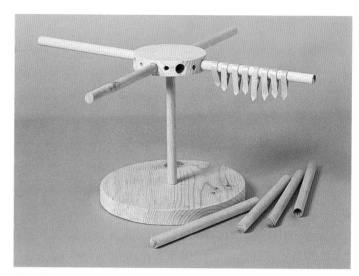

6 Ribbon loops on a drying rack

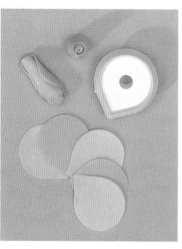

7 Rose blossom assembly

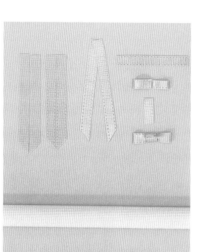

8 Bow stages

BOWS

15 Make the bows in the same way as for the ribbon strips (step 8). Fold two loops into the centre. Cover the join with a small strip and pinch in at the back (pic 8). If the paste is drying too quickly, moisten with a very little water. Cut the tails in pairs, making sure they are long enough to drape over the panels, and attach with edible gum glue. Secure the prepared bow loops at the top of the tails with gum glue.

FINISHING

16 Centre the bottom cake on the cake stand. Insert the centre post through the cake and attach it to the cake stand, then slip the moulded sugar vase over the top of it. Cover the join at the base with two little circles of soft lavender-blue flower paste/gum paste rope, and allow to dry. Fold a 5 x 65 cm/2 x 26 inch strip of soft lavender-blue sugarpaste/rolled fondant in half. Trim evenly using a ruler as a guide. Encircle the bottom cake and neatly join at the back. Pipe a small bead of royal icing to seal the join, and attach the bows to the edge of the cake board. Add the ribbon border to the top tier. Connect a custom-made 14 cm/5¹/₂ inch cake plate to the centre post above the separator. Carefully position the top tier after the cake is delivered to the reception site.

Glimpsed under Glass

CAKE AND DECORATION

- 15 cm/6 inch round cake
- Flower paste/gum paste (optional, for glass dome decoration)
- 850 g/1¾ lb sugarpaste/rolled fondant
- 2.5 ml/½ tsp Tylose powder/CMC (J)
- Pink, green and pale teal food colourings (VB/CK)
- Pale pink and buttercup petal dusts (VB/CK)
- Small moulded sugar vase (see pages 74–5)

EQUIPMENT

- 50 cm/20 inch reproduction glass dome
- Ribbon (optional, for glass dome decoration)
- Plastic lace, lace fabric or a lace press
- Rose cutter box base (OP) or paper template for cake plaque (see page 154)
- Rose leaf cutter (OP – R7) or any other small rose leaf cutter
- Small soft pointed paintbrush
- Veining tool
- Small and medium five-petal blossom cutters
- Miniature daisy cutter
- Throat tool
- Tiny leaf cutter (RVO)
- 15 cm/6 inch thin round cake board
- 25 cm/10 inch round cake board
- Celformer (CC)
- Rose petal cutter (OP – R2)
- Ball tool
- Plastic spoons
- 20-gauge wire
- Calyx cutter
- Floral tape
- Satay stick/bamboo skewer
- Lace edge cutter (FMM – M5)
- Small circular Lucite disk

THE ESSENCE OF ELEGANCE AND A CELEBRATION OF STYLE. CRISP PASTEL HIGHLIGHTS AND A SPLASH OF ROSES COMBINE WITH ROMANTIC VINCENT MARQUETRY. THIS TECHNIQUE CAN BE COMPARED WITH FRENCH FURNITURE INLAY – PATTERNS ARE FORMED BY THE INSERTION OF CUTTER LEAVES AND FLOWERS IN A SUGARPASTE VENEER. NEW MAGIC AT WORK WITH THE DOME PRESENTATION.

THE CAKE PLAQUE

1 Knead the Tylose powder into 250 g/8 oz sugarpaste/rolled fondant, then set aside for an hour to rest. Prepare separate walnut-sized balls of pink, green and white from the Tylose-strengthened paste. Colour the remaining strengthened paste with pale teal food colouring.

2 Roll out the pale teal sugarpaste/rolled fondant and emboss with plastic lace, lace fabric or a lace press. For this 15 cm/6 inch petal-shaped plaque, use the rose box base as a cutter or the paper template (see page 154) and cut the outline with a craft knife or

1 Creating the Vincent Marquetry cake plaque

scalpel. Gently pull the excess paste away. Immediately cut out the rose leaves, using the rose leaf cutter. Remove each leaf with the point of the craft knife or scalpel and replace it with a pale green, strengthened-paste replica. There is no need to add any moisture as the paste is self sticking. A small soft pointed paintbrush is useful to manoeuvre stubborn pieces into position. Vein the leaf with the veining tool. Repeat the process, cutting into the corners of the original leaf and being sure to overlap them, since this is part of the charm of this technique.

3 Make and add the flowers in the same way and in the following order. Cut and insert pale pink flowers into an empty spot of the same size, using the medium five-petal blossom cutter; then repeat this process with the white flowers, using

the small five-petal blossom cutter. Finish with the miniature white daisies, using the daisy cutter. Mark each flower with the throat tool and press the veining tool into its petals, to suggest movement (pic 1) – remembering the paste markings are difficult to correct later. It is a good idea for beginners to cover the parts not being worked on with plastic wrap, and lay a barely damp tea towel over the wrap, to avoid dry and brittle edges.

4 Complete the design with miniature leaf accents, cutting these with the tiny leaf cutter. Edge the plaque with strips of strengthened paste folded in half and attached with water to the underside of the plaque. Dry the decorated plaque thoroughly.

CAKE BOARD DECORATION

5 Cover the 25 cm/10 inch cake board with pale teal strengthened sugarpaste/rolled fondant. For the cake board decoration, repeat the same basic Vincent Marquetry method as used for the cake plaque, but varying the pattern (pic 2).

THE ROSE

6 Using an ice pick or knitting needle, pierce a hole through the base of the celformer, then line with greaseproof/wax paper. Prepare the centre cone and allow to dry. Cut out the first five rose petals with the rose petal cutter. Wrap the first pair beneath the cone. Add the next layer using the remaining three, then set aside. Cut four more sets of five rose petals. Thin the petal edges with the ball tool and brush them with pale pink petal dust, then highlight the base with buttercup petal dust. Press each petal into the palm of the hand, to vein it, then shape over the back

2 Close up of the Vincent Marquetry cake board

of a plastic spoon. Place the shaped petals in the celformer, working from the outside to the centre. Support each petal with a foam sponge, if necessary. Using royal icing, glue the petals in position, offsetting each petal from the one above it. Gently push the prepared centre through the rose and the celformer, and place over a cup to dry. Next day, make the calyx with the calyx cutter, nick and trim it (pic 3) and then attach around the base of the rose petals. Wire and floral tape the stem. For the leaves, see page 119.

3 Components for creating the roses

SIDE DECORATION

7 Centre the cake on the thin round cake board and then cover it with pale teal sugarpaste/rolled fondant, bringing the paste right down over the board edges. Centre on the inlaid cake board and attach with a little royal icing. Divide the cake in 3 cm/1¼ inch sections. Cut 10 x 3 cm/4 x 1¼ inch panels. Gather with the satay stick/bamboo skewer, then press down hard on to the non-stick board, to keep the ruched pleats together. Trim and neaten the edges with a craft knife

or scalpel. Attach the ruched pleated panels to the side and cover the joins with zig-zag strips of 5 mm/¼ inch pale teal paste made using the lace edge cutter (see page 144). Roll some pale teal paste into a long sausage and circle around the base of the cake. Make flowers with the small five-petal blossom cutter. Brush with pale pink petal dust and attach between the ruched pleated panels with royal icing.

FINISHING TOUCHES

8 Centre the plaque on the cake, supporting it with the Lucite disk so it just clears the tops of the panels. Fill a small moulded sugar vase with the sugar moulded roses and place on top. Measure the height of the cake and the flowers, and check to see there is room to fit everything under the dome. (The first time I did this, I misjudged the height and came very close to smashing every flower in the arrangement.) The illusion can be deceiving, the glass appears to be taller than it really is and one can be fooled into thinking there is plenty of room. It is also worth noting that the inside dimension is smaller than the outside. Carefully cover the cake and flowers with the glass dome.

A Jewel in the Crown

GUEST CAKE BY SCOTT FERGUSON

CAKE AND DECORATION

- 13 cm/5 inch round cake, 8 cm/3 inches deep; 20 cm/8 inch round cake, 10 cm/4 inches deep; and 30 cm/12 inch square cake, 13 cm/5 inches deep
- 1 kg/2 lb white chocolate (summer coat)
- 125 g/4 oz each white, ivory and dark peach flower paste/gum paste
- Silk-white and super pearl lustre dusts (VB/CK)
- 500 g/1 lb pale peach flower paste/gum paste
- Cosmos, orange, magenta and yellow petal dusts (VB/CK)
- 3.5 kg/7 lb ivory sugarpaste/rolled fondant
- 125 g/4 oz royal icing

EQUIPMENT

- Original elephant to be duplicated
- 1 kg/2 lb thixotropic silicone or kneadable silicone clay
- 2.5 mm/$\frac{1}{8}$ inch dowel rods
- Pointed tweezers
- Cold porcelain • Five-point throat tool
- Oval mould, domed in the centre
- Kingston cutter former (TOB)
- Lace leaf mould (ADM – LD300)
- Mexican hat pad (OP)
- Small circle cutter • White 30-gauge wire
- Templates (see page 158) • Sugarcraft gun
- Plunger cutters (FMM – LV1 and B1)
- Quick rose cutter (OP – F6)
- 13 cm/5 inch and 25 cm/10 inch round cake boards
- Peach ribbon, 5 mm/$\frac{1}{4}$ inch wide, to trim
- 5 mm/$\frac{1}{4}$ inch dowel rods
- Endless lace cutter (OP – LA1)
- 30 cm/12 inch square cake board

DELICATELY CARVED IVORY WITH THE ALLURING PERFUME OF JASMINE AND ROSES ARE SYMBOLIC OF THE ROMANTIC FAR EAST. UNDER AN EXQUISITE CANOPY, NOBLE CHOCOLATE ELEPHANTS OFFER FLOWER GARLANDS (MALAI) TO THE HONOURED BRIDAL COUPLE. WHO COULD RESIST THIS EXOTIC WEDDING CAKE?

DUPLICATING THE ELEPHANT

1 Mix the thixotropic silicone or kneadable silicone clay, as per the manufacturer's directions, and apply a smooth shell at least 5 mm/^{1}/4 in thick over the elephant to be duplicated. Using a craft knife or scalpel, cut the cured mould away, into three or more pieces (pic 1). Wash; dry then reassemble the mould, securing with rubber bands.

2 Melt the white chocolate (summer coat) as per the manufacturer's directions. Prop the mould upside down and pour the coating into each of the legs (pic 2), gently tapping to release any air. Insert 2.5 mm/^{1}/8 inch dowels into each leg while the coating is liquid. When cool, carefully remove the mould. Remove any seam marks with a knife, then polish with nylon ladies' stocking/hose.

1 Elephant and prepared silicone mould

CROWN FLOWERS

3 Modify the tweezers by moulding a small amount of cold porcelain around the tweezer points and forming two tiny, opposing, bean-shaped pads. Allow to harden thoroughly. Form a sausage shape from some white flower paste/gum paste, and insert the throat tool into one end. Clip indentations with scissors and pull each section into a rounded point (pic 3). Insert a cocktail stick/toothpick right through the sausage. Slightly dampen the back of each point and tightly roll under, into a volute. Roll the sausage between your fingers to form a ball and pinch off the excess paste. Using a palette knife, make vertical indentations between each volute. With the modified tweezers, pull out each section and form a dimple. When dry, remove from the cocktail stick/toothpick, and dust with silk-white lustre dust. Make one hundred crown flowers.

3 Stages of making the crown flowers

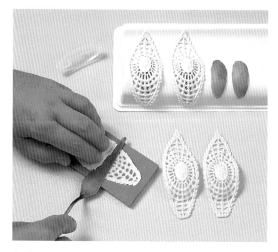

2 Pouring the white chocolate into the mould

LACE LEAVES

4 Wash the oval domed mould thoroughly and fill with remnant flower paste/gum paste. Level back, then remove the 'pad' from the mould, place it on the Kingston former, and allow to dry. Make eight such temporary support pads.

5 Using some stiff ivory flower paste/gum paste, work in more shortening and cornflour/cornstarch until the mixture slices easily. Dust the leaf lace mould with cornflour/cornstarch and press the paste into the mould. Slice off the excess paste with a palette knife (pic 4). Patch any holes, trimming a second time if needed. Remove the paste lace from the mould and place on the Kingston former, centring over a support pad. When dry, brush with super pearl lustre dust. Make twenty-eight lace leaves.

4 Removing the excess paste from a lace leaf

MINI BELLS

6 Press some white flower paste/gum paste into a hole on the Mexican hat pad and roll until the top is even and thin. Remove the paste from the pad, invert, neaten up, and cut with the circle cutter (pic 5). Insert dampened wire into the top of each 'bell' and allow to dry. Brush with silk-white lustre dust. Make twenty mini bells.

FRAMED FILIGREE PANELS

7 Tape greaseproof paper/wax paper over the filigree paper template (see page 158). With the ridged ribbon disk in the sugarcraft gun, form the frame with ivory flower paste/gum paste, mitring the edges and securing with water on an artist's brush (pic 6). Make four of these frames and allow to dry.

8 Cut out the filigree paper template. Prick each hole centre with a pin so you can feel it on the underside (like Braille). Roll a sheet of dark peach flower paste/gum paste with a pasta machine. Place the template over it and press lightly to transfer the dot grid on to the paste. Cut the perimeter of the template with a craft knife or scalpel, but do not remove the excess paste. Lift off the template. Centre the LV1 plunger cutter over each dot, cut and remove each flower, then remove the excess paste. Make four filigree panels. Using edible gum glue, attach the ivory frames to filigree panels. For the four teardrop shapes, repeat steps 7–8 but using the teardrop template (see page 158).

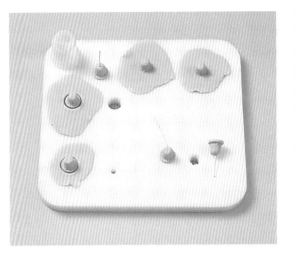

5 Creating the mini bells

> ## OTHER FLORAL DECORATIONS
>
> **9** Make 150 roses (see page 94) with pale peach flower paste/gum paste and the rose cutter, then paint them with cosmos, orange, magenta or yellow petal dusts mixed with clear alcohol. Make 100 jasmine finger flowers with white flower paste/gum paste, painting the centres with yellow petal dust. Insert 10 cm/4 inches of dampened wire into only twelve jasmine flowers.

ASSEMBLING THE TOP TIERS

10 Cover the two round cakes and matching boards with ivory sugarpaste/rolled fondant. Glue the peach ribbon to the larger cake board. Dowel and stack the top two tiers (see page 142). With royal icing, glue eleven lace leaves around the top tier and seventeen around the middle tier. Alternate jasmine and rose blossoms between the two tiers, and on the top dome. With the endless lace cutter, cut a lace strip in ivory paste and gum glue it over the ribbon. Insert bell wires under the lace. Trim each lace leaf with a small leaf and B1 plunger cutter.

THE BOTTOM TIER

11 Mitre the corners of the square cake, then place on its matching board and cover with ivory sugarpaste/rolled fondant. Insert 5 mm/¼ inch dowels into the cake at each elephant leg location. Gum glue the filigree panels to the cake sides.

12 String crown flowers on to wire and form loops and drops (see pic 3). Attach three drops to each loop. Support a floral garland on each elephant's trunk. Arrange the remaining roses around the base of the bottom cake and around the elephants.

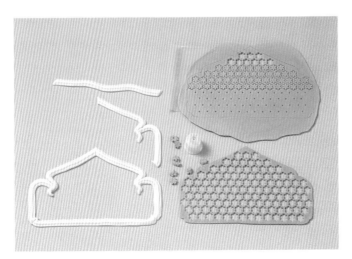

6 Components of the framed filigree panels

Affair with Blue and White

GUEST CAKE BY LOYDENE BARRETT

CAKE AND DECORATION

- 30 cm/12 inch and 25 cm/10 inch scalloped oval cakes
- 20 cm/8 inch oval cake
- 5 kg/10 lb white sugarpaste/rolled fondant
- Delphinium-blue and moss-green paste colourings (W)
- 750 g/1½ lb white flower paste/gum paste
- Buttercup-yellow, brown, moss-green, sage-green, forest-green and cinnamon petal dusts (VB/CK)
- Super pearl lustre dust

EQUIPMENT

- 45 x 40 cm/18 x 16 inch scalloped oval plywood cake board, 7.5 mm/³/8 inch deep
- 32 cm/13 inch oval cake board
- Starburst and small curved leaf cutwork cutters (EC)
- White 26- and 30-gauge wires
- Veining tool
- White stamens
- Celboard (CC)
- White ginger cutters (R)
- Orchid veiner (R)
- Ball tool
- Green floral tape
- Green 26-gauge wire
- Celstick (CC)
- 12 x 5 mm/¼ inch dowel rods
- Long sharpened dowel rod
- Round piping tube/tip (W – 2)
- Varipin/Rosa's Roller (OP)
- Freesia cutter
- Airpen syringe (SPC) or small piping bag
- 18 x 0 line brush
- 3 x 35 cm/14 inch lengths of plastic tubing, 5 mm/¼ inch wide

REFLECTING SUMMER SKIES AT THE HEIGHT OF THE WEDDING SEASON, THESE TIERS OF PRISTINE WHITE WITH DELPHINIUM-BLUE HIGHLIGHTS BLEND LACY CLASSIC DESIGN WITH CONTEMPORARY CHARM. ON THE CAKE, A STRIKING CONTRAST OF BLUE CUTWORK AND FRENCH KNOT DRAPES IS ACCENTED WITH SPRAYS OF WHITE GINGER AND ORCHIDS.

COVERING THE CAKE BOARD

1 Cut out the scalloped oval cake board from the plywood. Tint 1 kg/2 lb of sugarpaste/rolled fondant with delphinium-blue paste colouring. Roll it out and use to cover the scalloped board. Allow the board to dry for several days. Place the 32 cm/13 inch oval cake board on the scalloped board. Roll out 370 g/12 oz of white sugarpaste/rolled fondant and cut it to a scalloped shape before placing it over both cake boards. Working quickly, trim the white covering 5 mm/¼ inch from the edge of the blue board. Using the starburst and curved leaf cutters, cut out the design on the edge of the white sugarpaste/rolled fondant (pic 1).

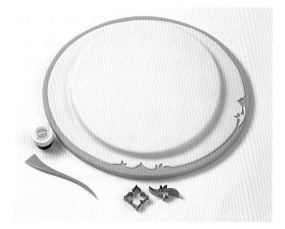

1 Decorating the paste-covered cake board

WHITE GINGER FLOWERS

2 Make the pistil by bending a small hook in a piece of white 30-gauge wire. Form a very small piece of white flower paste/gum paste similar in shape to a grain of rice. Insert the hook end of the wire into the 'grain of rice', positioning it close to one end. With the pointed end of the blade tool, make an indentation across the top. Insert a white stamen in the end away from the wire. When dry, brush with buttercup-yellow petal dust, then tint with brown petal dust on the top. Dust moss-green petal dust on the stamen.

3 Roll out a small ball of flower paste/gum paste on the celboard. Cut out one petal, using the round white ginger cutter. Moisten the white 26-gauge wire and insert into the ridge. Pinch the base close to the wire and lightly vein with the orchid veiner. Place the petal on the petal pad and soften its edges with the ball tool. Dry on ridged packing foam. Make and wire the remaining petals but vein only the oval ones. Using the oval white ginger cutter, cut one petal, then flip the cutter over and cut a second one, so there is a right and left oval petal. Finally cut three petals, using the narrow white ginger cutter, and fold in half lengthways. Colour the base, front and back of each petal with buttercup-yellow petal dust, and tint with moss-green petal dust (pic 2).

4 Bend the wire of the pistil in an S-shape. With one-third width of floral tape, bind the pistil to the round petal and then the three narrow petals. Position the oval petals between the narrow ones. Prepare seven more of these white ginger flowers, repeating steps 2–4.

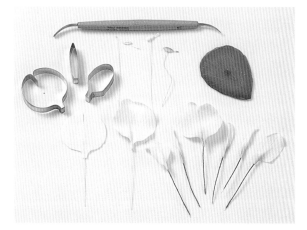

2 Creating the white ginger flowers

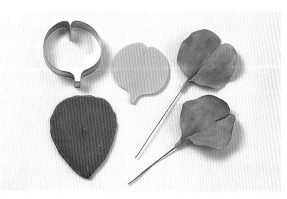

3 Making the white ginger leaves

LEAVES

5 Tint a small amount of flower paste/gum paste with moss-green paste colouring and roll out on the celboard. Cut out the leaves using the round white ginger cutter. Moisten the green 26-gauge wire and insert into the ridge. Place on the petal pad and soften its edges. Lightly vein with the orchid veiner. Pinch the leaf together up the centre, and dry on ridged packing foam. When dry, colour the leaf with sage-green and forest-green petal dusts. Brush stripes on the leaf surface with cinnamon petal dust, as well as the edges (pic 3). Prepare six more leaves.

FILLER ORCHIDS

6 Roll a pea-sized ball of white flowerpaste/gumpaste into a cone and hollow out with the celstick. Using small scissors, cut the cone into four equal petals. Cut two opposite petals in half, so there are two wide petals and four narrow ones. Thin all but one wide petal between your thumb and finger. Fold the outside edge of the thick petal into the centre and create a channel. Insert a stamen at an angle through the centre, and secure. Colour the centre buttercup-yellow and the base with moss-green petal dust. Make buds by inserting a moistened white 26-gauge wire into a pea-sized ball of paste, and dust each base with moss-green (pic 4).

4 Stages of making the filler orchids

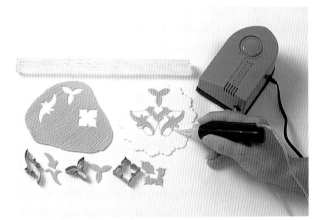

5 Assembling the cutwork design

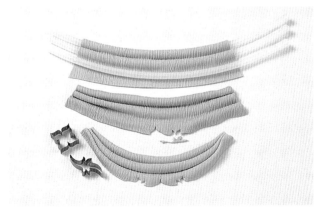

6 Creating the swags

7 Making the French knot drapes

STACKING THE CAKES

7 Cover the cakes with white sugarpaste/rolled fondant. Dowel and stack each one (see page 142). Pipe a snail trail around the base of each cake.

CUTWORK

8 Roll out some delphinium-blue sugarpaste/rolled fondant and texture with the Varipin/Rosa's Roller. Using the cutwork and freesia cutters, cut the paste (pic 5), moisten and position on the top and middle tiers. Fill the airpen syringe or small piping bag with royal icing and outline the cutwork pieces. Pipe royal icing from one piece to another until you have created the look of Belgian lace. After attaching each string, use the moistened line brush to neaten the joins.

SWAGS AND FRENCH KNOT DRAPES

9 Roll out some delphinium-blue sugarpaste/rolled fondant and texture with the Varipin/Rosa's Roller. Using a craft knife or scalpel, cut the swag. Space three lengths of plastic tubing 5 mm/¹/₄ inch apart and lay the textured paste over them. Squeeze the tubing together to gather up the paste swag. Using the starburst and small curved leaf cutters, cut out the swag edge. Remove the tubing, pinch the ends together (pic 6), moisten and position on the cakes.

10 For the drop, roll out the remaining blue paste and texture with the Varipin/Rosa's Roller. Cut out a flared piece 6 cm/2¹/₂ inches long. Gather at the narrow edge, moisten and attach at the end of each swag. For the knot, cut out a 5 x 2.5 cm/2 x 1 inch rectangle (pic 7). Shape and gather into a knot; position over the drop. Brush the entire cake with super pearl lustre dust.

Invitation to a Summer Wedding

GUEST CAKE BY CAROLYN WANKE

CAKE AND DECORATION

- 18 cm/7 inch, 28 cm/11 inch and 38 cm/15 inch round cakes
- 90 g/3 oz each pink and egg-yellow flower paste/gum paste
- 5.5 kg/11 lb white sugarpaste/ rolled fondant
- 55 g/2 oz white flower paste/gum paste
- 270 g/9 oz green sugarpaste/rolled fondant

EQUIPMENT

- Teardrop rose cutters (2.3 cm/⁷/₈ inch and 2.8 cm/1¹/₈ inch)
- Ball tool
- Petal pad
- 2 baroque moulds
- Paper templates for the baroque pieces (see page 158)
- 5 cm/2 inch square cutter
- Aluminium flashing
- Basketweave rolling pin (PME)
- 5 mm/¹/₄ inch wooden skewer
- Wooden cushion nail
- Reusable adhesive
- Piping tubes/tips (W – 4, 349)
- 45 cm/18 inch round plywood cake board
- 140 cm/56 inches braid or ribbon, 1.5 cm/⁵/₈ inches wide, to trim board
- Glue gun
- 18 cm/7 inch, 28 cm/11 inch and 38 cm/15 inch thin round cake boards
- 10 x 5 mm/¹/₄ inch dowel rods
- Long sharpened dowel

SEARCHING FOR A SPECIAL CAKE, THE BRIDE-TO-BE WOULD NOT BE DISAPPOINTED WITH THIS PRETTY DESIGN, ESPECIALLY SUITED TO A SUMMER WEDDING. WHIMSICIAL BASKETS FILLED WITH MINIATURE ROSES REFLECTING RAINBOW HUES ARE PULLED TOGETHER WITH TWISTED SUGAR RIBBONS. ROMANTIC BLISS INDEED!

THE ROSES

1 For each closed bud, roll out coloured flower paste/gum paste and cut with the appropriately sized teardrop cutter. Thin the petal edges using the ball tool and petal pad. Roll the petal into a tight bud, lengthening the bottom portion to form a solid pointed stem (pic 1). Make 140 small buds and thirty large buds of each colour. Dry completely. Set aside sixty small buds of each colour.

2 For each open bud, lighten the coloured flower paste/gum paste with same amount of white flower paste/gum paste. Repeat step 1 for rolling, cutting and thinning petals. Wrap two or three petals around each of the remaining buds to make an open bud.

3 For the open rose, use six small open buds and thirty large open buds of each colour. Repeat step 2 for colouring the flower paste/gum paste, rolling, cutting and thinning petals. Add five petals to each open bud to form the rose.

1 Stages of the rose blossoms

2 Making the basketweave cones

TOP BAROQUE PIECES

4 Press white sugarpaste/rolled fondant into the two baroque moulds, unmould and trim to fit the paper templates (see page 158). Glue the two sides back to back with white royal icing, and trim the edges to match. Make three double pieces and allow to dry.

BASKETWEAVE CONES AND BOWS

5 Cut six 9 x 15 cm/3³⁄₈ x 6 inch pieces of aluminium flashing and fold the 15 cm/6 inch side in half to a 90 degree angle. Cut six 8 x 15 cm/3 x 6 inch pieces of greaseproof/wax paper and fold in half. Roll out 55 g/ 2 oz white sugarpaste/rolled fondant to 2 mm/¹⁄₁₆ inch thick, with the basketweave rolling pin. Cut three squares, positioning the cutter so that the weave goes from corner to corner; then cut each square in half on the horizontal weave line. Form a cone with each triangle and flatten the seam by rolling with the wooden skewer. Trim top points, leaving just enough paste to fold over the corner of the flashing. Thin and flare the top edge of each cone by gently pinching. Dry overnight on the flashing (pic 2).

6 When dry, attach a 4.5 mm/³⁄₁₆ inch, white flower paste/gum paste ribbon, 5.5 cm/2¹⁄₄ inches long, around each cone 1 cm/¹⁄₂ inch from top.

7 Secure the flashing to the cushion nail with a small amount of reusable adhesive. Use royal icing to attach greaseproof/wax paper to the flashing, the cone on to the greaseproof/wax paper, and the roses in the cone.

Cut rose stems as required. Hold the cushion nail and turn or twist the nail to get the proper angles for piping leaves, with green royal icing and the No.349 piping tube/tip. Release the flashing from the cushion nail by holding it on either side of the bend and gently moving from side to side. Set aside for the icing to dry. Repeat step 7 for each of the remaining five cones.

8 Make six small bows, 2 cm/³/₄ inches wide, in white flower paste/gum paste, and allow to dry.

PREPARING THE CAKES

9 Cover the 45 cm/18 inch cake board with white sugarpaste/rolled fondant and attach ribbon or trim around the edge of the board with the glue gun. Place cooled cakes on matching-sized thin cake boards and cover with paste. Cut dowels to the cake heights and insert into the two bottom tiers (see page 142). Stack the cakes on the covered cake board, securing with royal icing and the long sharpened dowel.

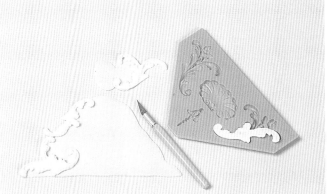

3 Creating the baroque pieces

BAROQUE TRIM

10 Customize paper templates for the baroque trim (see page 158) by measuring one-sixth the circumference of your cake by its height. Line up and mark the base of each tier in sixths. For the bottom tier, press four white sugarpaste/rolled fondant pieces in the baroque mould, and trim to match (pic 3). Place greaseproof/wax paper over the paper template panel and form paste pieces to fit in the space. Arrange five more sets of baroque pieces on greaseproof/wax paper and freeze all until needed. Use the same technique for the top tier.

UNDERLAY PIECES

11 Draw paper templates for the underlays (see page 158). Roll out green sugarpaste/rolled fondant, transfer to greaseproof/wax paper, place the template on top, and cut to shape with a sharp craft knife or scalpel. Mark the centre bottom of each underlay for the bottom tier. Freeze until needed. Cut six underlays for the bottom tier and six for the top tier.

FINISHING

12 As each underlay is removed from the freezer, match the underlay centre mark with the cake mark on the bottom tier, and attach. For the top tier, place the centre of the piece 2.5 cm/1 inch above the cake mark. With the No.4 piping tube/tip, pipe royal icing at the base of each tier. Using royal icing, attach each set of baroque pieces over the edges of the underlays, fasten the three baroque pieces to the top tier, and secure the basketweave cones to the middle tier. Place large roses on the top cake and at the base of the bottom tier. Use the small roses to fill in and complete the arrangements. Pipe green royal icing leaves with the No.349 piping tube/tip. Join the cones with 4.5 mm/³/₁₆ inch strips of twisted, white flower paste/gum paste. To finish, attach streamers, 10 cm/4 inches and 13 cm/5 inches long, and paste bows to each cone.

Here Comes the Groom

GUEST CAKE BY MAXINE BOYINGTON

WHILE THE GROOM'S CAKE IS CONSIDERED TO BE A SOUTHERN AMERICAN TRADITION, IT IS FAST GAINING POPULARITY IN OTHER AREAS. IT HAS GONE THROUGH MANY INCARNATIONS, FROM A SMALL PIECE OF CAKE PACKED IN A BOX GIVEN TO THE GUEST TO TAKE HOME, TO ITS MOST POPULAR FORM TODAY – A RICH CHOCOLATE CAKE WITH CHOCOLATE ICING.

CAKE AND DECORATION
- 40 x 31 cm/16 x 12¹/₂ inch oval cake
- 125 g/4 oz each very pale green and mid-brown flower paste/gum paste
- Moss-green, golden-yellow, brown and dark green petal dusts (VB/CK)
- 500 g/1 lb white flower paste/gum paste
- Green, brown, black and yellow airbrush colours
- Black, brown and moss-green paste food colourings (VB/CK)
- 1 kg/2 lb brown pastillage (see page 134)
- 250 g/8 oz Chinese rice noodles/cellophane noodles/rice sticks
- Green, brown, black and white powdered candy colours (VB/CK)
- 2.5 kg/5 lb chocolate-brown sugarpaste/rolled fondant
- 250 g/8 oz ivory sugarpaste/rolled fondant

EQUIPMENT
- White 18- and 20-gauge wires
- Brown floral tape • Angled tweezers
- Pale gold embroidery floss
- Heavy cardboard, 4 cm/1¹/₂ inches wide
- Paper templates (see page 152)
- Leaf board
- Applecrate/apple box divider
- Veining tool
- Bubble foam or eggcrate foam
- Airbrush • Wire coat hanger
- Heavy aluminium foil • Wire brush
- 55 x 45 cm/22 x 18 inch polystyrene/styrofoam board, 5 cm/2 inch thick
- 40 x 31 cm/16 x 12¹/₂ inch oval sturdy board
- 55 x 45 cm/22 x 18 inch oval heavy board
- Fabric covering for cake board (EM)
- Biscuit/cookie press • Sugarcraft gun

MAGNOLIA CENTRES

1 Roll a ball of the very pale green flower paste/gum paste, then taper it into a slightly rounded cone (pic 1). Cut three pieces of 18-gauge wire, one being slightly longer than the other two. Bend a hook in the longer piece and bind all three wires together with the floral tape. Dip the wire in edible gum glue and insert securely into the base of the cone. Using fine scissors and beginning about two-thirds of the way down the cone, make fine cuts moving towards the point of the cone. After every few cuts, carefully curl the ends down. Then, using angled tweezers, pinch vertical lines on the lower third of the cone. With fine scissors, clip the top half of each of these lines, so they flare out slightly from the cone but should not curl back. Allow the cone to dry thoroughly.

1 Making the magnolia flower centres

2 Wind the embroidery floss 8–10 times around heavy cardboard. Carefully slip the floss off the cardboard, wire the centre and cut all loops. Moisten with gum glue, and spread the 'stamens' apart. Two of these will be needed for each flower. Place on each side of the central cone and bind with floral tape. Trim to just slightly larger than the cone base. Dust between the curled points with moss-green petal dust. Dust the curled points and the extensions at the cone base with golden-yellow petal dust. Add a touch of brown to the tips of the curls. The more open the flower, the darker these curls.

MAGNOLIA PETALS

3 Magnolias normally have nine petals, in three sizes. For the inner petal, put a slight curve into the end of a piece of white 20-gauge wire. Roll the white flower paste/gum paste on the leaf board and cut three petals with the craft knife or scalpel, using the inner petal template (see page 152). With a large ball tool, thin the petal edges, being careful not to ruffle them more than necessary. Using the ball tool or the rounded end of a rolling pin, work the inside of the petal to begin cupping it. Pinch a small pleat at the tip of the petal. Insert the prepared wire into the ridge made by the leaf board. Taper the end of the petal around the wire and lay the petal in the former, to obtain the desired shape, forcing the centre down and being sure that the curved part of the wire follows the curve of the petal. (A divider used in apple-crates/apple boxes makes a good former.) Make three middle and three outer petals in the same way.

4 Attach the petals to the flower centre with the floral tape, placing the inner ones equidistant around the cone, the middle petals between the inner ones, and the outer petals behind the inner petals (pic 2). Thicken the magnolia stems with extra wire or several layers of floral tape, until they are the desired width.

2 Stages of the magnolia petals

MAGNOLIA LEAVES

5 Magnolia leaves are large and fairly straight, with a definite curve at the centre vein and slight curves under at the edge. They are glossy dark green on top and soft brown underneath. Darken the green flower paste/gum paste, then roll it and mid-brown paste together on the largest slot on the leaf board, with the brown side facing down. Cut the leaf with a craft knife, using either leaf template (see page 152). Place the brown side up on a soft pad and thin the edges with the ball tool – this will also create a gentle curve under the leaf edge. Since most commercial leaf veiners are not large enough for these leaves, use the veining tool to mark the veins in the leaves. Make a sharp crease down the centre and insert a piece of 20-gauge wire. Place the leaf on bubble foam or eggcrate foam, positioning it so that the centre is between the bubbles and the outside edges curve over them. When completely dry, dust the leaf underside with brown petal dust, using a wide soft brush, and then lightly with cornflour/cornstarch, to give the velvety look of a natural leaf. Dust or airbrush the green side with dark green petal dust or green airbrush colour (pic 3), then make the green side glossy by holding the completely dried leaf over a steaming kettle.

3 Preparing the magnolia leaves

MAKING THE LOG

6 Build the log on a wire armature such as a wire coat hanger, bending it to the desired shape and building up the design with heavy aluminium foil. Cover with the brown pastillage. As long as the foil doesn't show through, don't worry about any cracks in the pastillage – they will lend more authenticity to the look of the log. Use the wire brush to add extra graining to the log. Also add knots and smaller stems, as desired. Dry thoroughly, and then airbrush with very dark brown, possibly with some black added. Spray this on, then wipe with a kitchen paper towel. This will leave the dark colour in the cracks and give more dimension to the log. Airbrush the log with a paler brown airbrush colour, and possibly some green and yellow airbrush colour, to create the desired look (pic 4).

4 Airbrushing colour into the log

SPANISH MOSS

7 Boil water in a saucepan, then add some black, brown and moss-green food colourings. Place the rice noodles/cellophane noodles/rice sticks in the boiling water for just a minute or two, until they are soft. Remove and spread out on kitchen paper towels to dry – this can take up to a day, at room temperature.

8 Mix the desired 'moss' colour using green, brown and black powdered candy colours. When the noodles are almost dry, sprinkle the powder mix over and through them, until they look like natural Spanish moss (pic 5). White powdered candy colour may need to be added to get the desired colour. Remove as much excess powder colour as possible. If the 'moss' is to be placed on a

5 Making Spanish moss

surface other than sugarpaste/rolled fondant, move it at this point, while not quite dry. Any moss that is going to touch sugarpaste/rolled fondant must be completely dry or it will mark the paste. For a specific shape, such as moss draping over the edge of the cake, use a cake tin/cake pan as a former.

6 A rope border made using a sugarcraft gun

ASSEMBLING THE CAKE

9 Bevel the polystyrene/styrofoam at the top, then set on the 55 cm/ 22 inch heavy board. Gather the fabric cover, at the top and bottom, with elastic, and pull over the prepared base board. (To order instructions for this base, see page 159, Earlene Moore.) Place the oval cake on the matching-sized, sturdy board. Cover with chocolate sugarpaste/rolled fondant, and centre on the fabric-covered base.

10 For the rope border, push ivory sugarpaste/rolled fondant through a biscuit/cookie press, or roll freehand. Twist two 'rope' pieces together, and cut the ends on a diagonal (pic 6). For the tassels, press ivory paste through the sugarcraft gun using the die with many small holes. To cover the seam where the tassels join the rope, make a small string with the single-holed die on the gun, then wrap it over the join.

Fantasia Roseta Romántica

GUEST CAKE BY ROSA VIACAVA DE ORTEGA

CAKE AND DECORATION

- 15 cm/6 inch, 20 cm/8 inch, 25 cm/10 inch and 30 cm/12 inch round cakes
- 500 g/1 lb white flower paste/gum paste
- White sparkle dust (VB/CK)
- Pink and lime petal dusts (VB/CK)
- Rose buds and leaves (see pages 94 and 119)
- Filler flowers
- 3.5 kg/7 lb white sugarpaste/rolled fondant
- 1.5 kg/3 lb white flower paste/gum paste and white sugarpaste/rolled fondant in a 50:50 mixture

EQUIPMENT

- 26-gauge wire
- Jasmine cutter and veiner mould (RVO – F108)
- Sponge foam
- Petal pad
- Ball tool
- Former
- Cake boards (see step 3)
- 3 mm beadmaker (CK)
- Dotted Swiss rolling pin (RVO – F33)
- Lace cutter (RVO – F06)
- 5 x foam twisty hair rollers or 1 cm/1/2 inch plastic tubing
- Large and medium fantasy leaf cutters (RVO) or paper templates (see page 157)
- Round piping tube/tip (W – 3)
- Lace rolling pin (RVO – F32)
- Kitchen paper towel tube former
- Separated cake stand (HD – Nancy)

TOUCHED WITH A SENSE OF PURE FANTASY, THIS EXQUISITELY CRAFTED WEDDING PRESENTATION IS TRULY A BRIDE'S DELIGHT. A DREAMY WHITE CLOUD GLISTENS WITH SPARKLING ACCENTS, WHITE BOWS AND UNIQUE LEAF OVERLAYS. TULLE BILLOWS AND SWIRLS BENEATH EACH CAKE, CREATING THE ILLUSION THAT THEY ARE SUSPENDED IN AIR.

FANTASY FLOWERS

1 For the flower centre, hook the 26-gauge wire and dip in edible gum glue. Attach a flat-topped teardrop of flower paste/gum paste to the wire. Brush with white sparkle dust and leave to dry. Prepare a Mexican hat in paste. Brush the jasmine cutter and veiner mould with white sparkle dust and press the Mexican hat into the mould. Trim the petal edges with the sponge, then remove the flower from the mould. Place on the petal pad and soften the edge with the ball tool. Push the flower centre through the flower, attaching with edible gum glue. Brush the flower with pink and lime petal dusts (pic 1), then place in the former to dry.

2 Make up four top posies, using a variety of small pink rose buds, fantasy flowers, filler flowers and rose leaves.

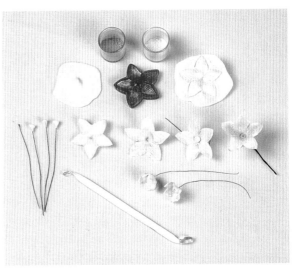

1 Follow these steps for the fantasy flowers

CAKE SIZE	BOARDS
15 cm/6 inch	18 cm/7 inch and 20 cm/8 inch
20 cm/8 inch	23 cm/9 inch and 25 cm/10 inch
25 cm/10 inch	28 cm/11 inch and 30 cm/12 inch
30 cm/12 inch	32.5 cm/13 inch and 35 cm/14 inch

PREPARING THE CAKES

3 Cover each cake with white sugarpaste/rolled fondant. Glue two boards together for each cake (see box, left). Cover the combined boards with paste, taking it over the edges. Centre the cakes on the boards and attach. Brush the inside of the beadmaker with white sparkle dust. Press flower paste/gum paste into the mould, then firmly push a rolling pin over the beadmaker. Open the mould and carefully remove the pearls (see page 54). Attach pearls to the base of each cake and to the second tier of each board.

RUCHED DRAPES

4 Roll out a 25 x 13 cm/10 x 5 inch strip of 50:50 mixture of flower paste/gum paste and sugarpaste/rolled fondant

2 Preparing the ruched drapes

using the dotted Swiss rolling pin. Create a decorative edge with the lace cutter, then remove the centre of each scallop. Lay each piece over the foam hair rollers or plastic tubing, forming folds by gathering at the top (pic 2). Leave to firm up. Attach to the top of the cake, using edible gum glue, drape over the sides and plump the drapes to create a ruched effect.

FANTASY LEAVES

5 Roll out more 50:50 mixture of flower paste/gum paste and sugarpaste/rolled fondant using the dotted Swiss rolling pin. With the fantasy leaf cutters, cut out large and medium leaves from the embossed paste, then brush with white sparkle dust. Using the piping tube/tip, create an open-work edge around each leaf (pic 3). Gather the top of each leaf into two folds. Overlap the drapes with the leaves, supporting with the sponge foam until dry.

3 Fantasy leaves with matching cutters

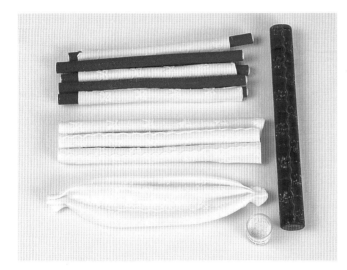

4 First stages of making the bow loops

BOWS AND RIBBON TAILS

6 Prepare a 23 x 13 cm/9 x 5 inch strip of 50:50 mixture of flower paste/gum paste and sugarpaste/rolled fondant, with the lace rolling pin. Using the foam hair rollers or plastic tubing, make three folds. Remove the rollers and pinch the paste at each end (pic 4). Bend each folded paste piece over a tube former and pinch together, to make the bow loops. Leave until dry (pic 5). Decorate each cake as illustrated and arrange on the cake stand.

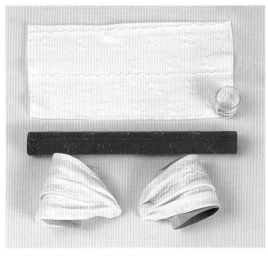

5 Second stages of the bow loops

Simply Pretty in Pink

CAKE AND DECORATION

- 15 cm/6 inch, 20 cm/8 inch and
  25 cm/10 inch round cakes
- 10 g/$^1/_3$ oz white flower paste/gum paste
- Purple and lime petal dusts (VB/CK)
- Purple and pale leaf-green powdered food
  colourings (VB/CK)
- Fine polenta/cornmeal
- 3.5 kg/7 lb pale pink sugarpaste/rolled
  fondant
- 500 g/1 lb white sugarpaste/rolled fondant
- Super pearl, avocado and silk-white lustre
  dusts (VB/CK)
- 55 g/2 oz pale pink flower paste/gum paste
- 10 g/$^1/_3$ oz green flower paste/gum paste
- One large rose, 10 cm/4 inches across
  (see page 106)

EQUIPMENT

- Ball tool
- Trumpet modelling tool (J)
- 18 x 0 line brush
- 28-gauge wire
- Floral tape
- 15 cm/6 inch, 20 cm/8 inch and
  25 cm/10 inch thin round cake boards
- 30 cm/12 inch round cake board
- Dowelling (see page 142)
- Sharp knife
- Round piping tube/tip (W – 1)
- Daisy centre mould (J)
- Rose leaf cutter (OP – R5)
- Veining tool
- Small and medium blossom cutters (OP –
  F2S and F2M; RVO or PME)

SIMPLE IN DESIGN, THIS CAKE HAS VISUAL IMPACT. PERFECT FOR A SMALL WEDDING, OR SUMMER BRIDAL TEA, IT IS DECORATED WITH AMERICAN VIOLETS, NOT THE TRADITIONAL ENGLISH VARIETY. TOPPED WITH A SUPERB FULL-BLOWN, OLD-FASHIONED ROSE, THE DRAPE TWISTS DOWN THE SIDE OF THE CAKE, ACCENTING THE OFFSET PLEATED JABOT BEFORE CURLING ON TO THE SERVING BOARD.

THE VIOLETS

1 Prepare a Mexican hat with white flower paste/gum paste and cut into five points using the scissors (pic 1). Thin the petals with a ball tool. The upper pair will be wider and longer than the rest; the lower outside set curled forward, then backward; and the central base petal, which is more square, is cupped forward.

2 Deepen the throat of the flower with the trumpet modelling tool. Brush the entire flower, except the throat, with purple petal dust. Tint the throat with lime petal dust. With the line brush, paint some fine dark purple lines at the base of the throat, using clear alcohol/vodka or Everclear mixed with purple food colouring.

3 Insert two tiny white ball-shaped flower paste/gum paste stamens at the front and dust with a little sifted polenta/cornmeal. Add a hooked 28-gauge wire, and bind with floral tape. Paint the calyx with alcohol-diluted, leaf-green food colouring. Dry.

1 Freehand violets and colouring procedure

PREPARING THE CAKES

4 Freeze the cakes before sculpting. Gradually and evenly sculpt 2.5 cm/ 1 inch away from the base of each cake, using a wide-bladed knife (see page 140). (The tops will still be at the original measurement but the bases will have decreased by 2.5 cm/1 inch.) Centre the cakes on the matching-sized thin cake boards. Cover with pale pink sugarpaste/ rolled fondant.

ROLLED STRIPS

5 Cut out continuous rolled strips, alternating pale pink and white sugarpaste/rolled fondant. Starting at the top edge of each cake and working towards the base, attach with a little edible gum glue (pic 2). Do not panic if each roll is not exactly even; they are meant to be slightly varied.

ROLLED STRIP GUIDE

Approximate circumference measurements for each cake:

15 cm/6 inch = 50 cm/20 inch strips

20 cm/8 inch = 65 cm/26 inch strips

25 cm/10 inch = 80 cm/32 inch strips

Make each strip approximately 6 cm/2½ inch wide, then fold in half.

6 Cover the 30 cm/12 inch cake board with a thin layer of pale pink sugarpaste/rolled fondant. Beginning at the edge of the board and working towards the centre, add continuous paste strips, making the first strip 100 cm/40 inches long, then reducing the strip length by 5–8 cm/2–3 inches each time as you progress towards the centre. Continue until about 10 cm/ 4 inches in depth from the edge has been covered. Brush all the rolled strips with super pearl lustre dust.

CAKE ASSEMBLY

7 Centre the bottom tier cake on the 30 cm/ 12 inch cake board. Add the other tiers, centring and dowelling each time (see page 142). Using the piping tube/tip, pipe a snail trail of royal icing or buttercream, to seal the cake edges, then add another continuous strip to cover the join, which should be offset to the left front.

2 Applying the rolled strips to the cake side

PLEATED RUFFLES

8 Cut 2.5 cm/1 inch strips of pale pink paste. Prepare a double pleated ruffle (pic 3) and attach over the rolled strip joins. Add a plain paste strip; make buttons in the daisy centre mould and brush with super pearl.

4 Rose leaves and cutter

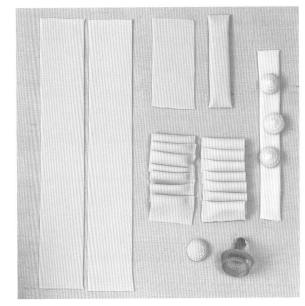

3 Stages of making the pleated ruffles

CAKE DRAPE

9 Roll out two 45 cm/18 inch strips of pale pink flower paste/gum paste, pinch in two pockets, then drape and twist down the side of the cake. Attach only at the centre of the top cake.

ROSE LEAVES

10 Cut out ten rose leaves from the green flower paste/gum paste, using the rose leaf cutter. Vein each leaf and brush with avocado lustre dust (pic 4). Dry two of them within the pockets of the drape so they will fit.

5 Stages of the filler flowers

6 Attaching the full-length drape

FILLER FLOWERS

11 Right at the last moment, just before they are needed, make the filler flowers in pale pink flower paste/gum paste, using the small and medium blossom cutters (pic 5). Cut out as many as required, cup with the veining tool, and brush with silk-white lustre dust.

FINISHING OFF

12 Slip the violets and rose leaves in the pockets created in the folds, and glue scattered filler blossoms down the drape (pic 6). Attach the large rose on top, then tuck rose leaves beneath it, securing with royal icing. Decorate the serving table with a circle of ruched silk fabric. Position the cake, then scatter paste violets and leaves on the fabric.

Love is in the Air

CAKE DECORATION

- 10 cm/4 inch, 15 cm/6 inch and 20 cm/8 inch round cakes
- 5 ml/1 tsp Tylose powder/CMC (J)
- 2 kg/4 lb pale teal sugarpaste/rolled fondant
- Antique silk lustre dust (VB/CK)
- Cornflour/cornstarch

EQUIPMENT

- 10 cm/4 inch, 15 cm/6 inch and 20 cm/8 inch thin round cake boards
- 25 cm/10 inch cake board
- Pale teal ribbon, 1.5 cm/⁵⁄₈ in wide, to trim cake board
- Open scalloped crimper (PME)
- Double-sided, saw-edged open scalloped crimper (PME)
- Adding machine tape
- Dotted Swiss rolling pin (RVO – F33)
- Lace cutter (FMM – M7)
- Broderie anglais cutter (PME)
- Floral rose posy mould (SB – 7865)
- 10 x 5 mm/¹⁄₄ inch dowel rods
- Long sharpened dowel rod
- Paintbrush
- Garrett frill cutter (OP – GF1) or any round, scallop-edged, 9 cm/3¹⁄₂ inch cutter such as scone or biscuit/ cookie cutter
- Plastic parasol bridal ornament

BRODERIE ANGLAIS — THE MOST FEMININE OF LACES — IS SEEN HERE IN A NEW LIGHT. UPDATED IN SOFTEST TEAL, WITH SOPHISTICATED, HAND-PAINTED, ANTIQUE SILK EYELETS, IT IS THE STUFF OF DAYDREAMS. BRIDES WILL BE ENCHANTED WITH THE SIMPLICITY OF THIS DRESDEN EFFECT. AN EPICUREAN MOMENT OF UNABASHED GLAMOUR FOR THE PERFECT FINISHING TOUCH.

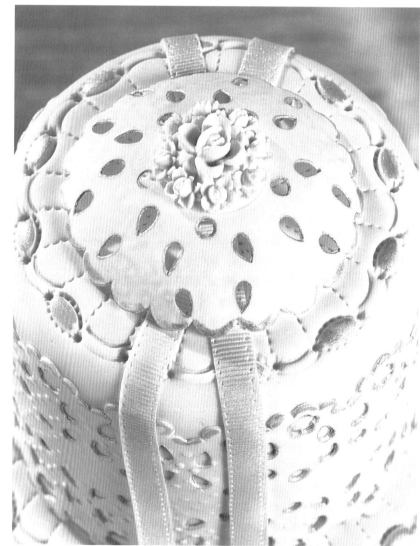

PREPARING THE DECORATION

1 Add the Tylose powder to 250 g/8 oz sugarpaste/rolled fondant and knead thoroughly. Cover well with plastic wrap and set aside for a couple of hours. Knead again before using this strengthened paste.

2 Centre each cake on its matching sized board. Trim the 25 cm/10 inch cake board with the ribbon and cover with unstrengthened paste. Then cover all the cakes with more of this paste. Embellish the paste edges, alternating the two crimpers (pic 1). Paint every second crimped space with antique silk lustre mixed with clear alcohol/vodka or Everclear. Once the bottom tier paste has firmed up, centre it on the cake board.

1 Sample of the scalloped design

2 Creating the eyelet flounce

BOTTOM TIER

3 For the base flounce, run a strip of the adding machine tape around the bottom tier cake, marking a line of pinpricks at the top. Roll fairly thin strips of the strengthened sugarpaste/rolled fondant – these were 6 x 30 cm/2$^{1}/_{2}$ x 12 inches. Emboss with the dotted Swiss rolling pin (pic 2). Enhance the edge using the lace cutter, then add extra decorative touches with the broderie anglais cutter. Check that the paste flounce is the same depth as the adding machine tape. Remove all the little eyelet pieces, using the point of a craft knife or scalpel. (These can be saved and recycled later for other projects requiring a raised embroidery pattern.) Circle the holes with antique silk lustre dust mixed with clear alcohol/vodka or Everclear. Once the alcohol has evaporated – after a minute or two – gather and attach the flounce to the cake, hanging it from the line of pinpricks. Make the second row much shorter, measuring the depth from the edge of the cake and overlapping the base flounce but not covering the eyelets. Proceed in the same manner as the base flounce but using the shorter depth – the depth was only 4 cm/ 1$^{1}/_{2}$ inches on this cake.

4 Trim the top edge with a double folded swag and tidy up with a dainty textured bow (pic 3), both made with the strengthened paste. Cover the join with a rose posy, also made with this paste and the floral posy mould. Dowel and stack the cakes (see page 142), using five dowels per cake, finishing with the long sharpened dowel.

SECOND TIER AND TOP TIER

5 Note the depth and circumference of both the second and top tiers. Add a 2.5 cm/1 inch overlap to the circumference measurement, for a clean cut. For the second tier, roll out the strengthened sugarpaste/rolled fondant. Emboss with the dotted Swiss rolling pin. Cut a lace edge on both sides using the lace cutter, plus a double row with the broderie anglais cutter. Make

OPTION FOR A LARGER CAKE

Add two flounced tiers at the base of a five-tier cake, with three wrapped tiers above.

sure the measurement corresponds to the depth at the greatest point. Paint the eyelets with the antique silk medium. Once the paint is dry, attach the strip to the cake so it is slightly off-centre at the back, using the barest amount of boiled water on a paintbrush and taking care not to distort the eyelets. For the top tier, repeat step 5.

6 Cover the joins with grosgrain ribbon (made from sugarpaste/rolled fondant), 5 mm/¼ inch wide (pic 4), draping it all the way from the top centre of the top tier to the top edge of the bottom tier cake. Attach another ribbon of similar length, offsetting it the same distance to the

HELP FOR BEGINNERS

The side design can be added before the stacking process, just in case some might feel nervous handling large pieces at a height.

left. Gently push the ribbons into the waist of the cake with the fingertips. Make a large posy from the strengthened paste, using the floral rose posy mould, and attach with edible gum glue so it keeps the ribbons correctly positioned. Add smaller, single moulded roses to the base of the tails.

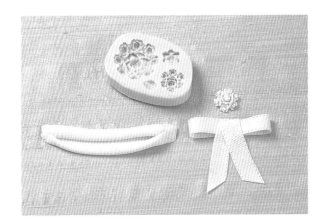

3 Swag, bow and rose posy

4 Grosgrain ribbons and rose posy

DOME CENTREPIECE

7 Cut out a circle from sugarpaste/rolled fondant, with the Garrett frill cutter or other scalloped-edged cutter. Divide the circle evenly and cut eyelets with the broderie anglais cutter (pic 5). Lightly dust a plastic parasol bridal ornament with cornflour/cornstarch and place the paste over it. When completely dry, paint the eyelets with antique silk lustre dust mixed with clear alcohol/vodka or Everclear. Centre the dome centrepiece on the top tier, attaching with edible gum glue or, for a perfect match, dissolve a pea-sized ball of strengthened sugarpaste/rolled fondant in a few drops of hot water for two seconds in the microwave and use this to attach the centrepiece. Add a moulded rose posy on top. The cake also looks good from the side and can be displayed that way if preferred.

5 Stages of the dome centrepiece

Breathtaking in Bride's Lace

CAKE AND DECORATION

- 15 cm/6 inch, 20 cm/8 inch, 25 cm/10 inch and 35 cm/14 inch oval cakes
- 55 g/2 oz white flower paste/gum paste
- Moss-green, brown and lime-green petal dusts (VB/CK)
- 5 ml/1 tsp fine polenta/cornmeal
- 15 g/½ oz green flower paste/gum paste
- Super pearl lustre dust (VB/CK)
- 7 kg/14 lb white sugarpaste/rolled fondant

EQUIPMENT

- 18- and 28-gauge wires
- Green floral tape
- Large rose petal cutter or paper template for lisianthus (see page 155)
- Ball tool
- Celformer (CC)
- Sponge foam
- Calyx cutter
- Lace medallion cutter (ELI – 501)
- Rounded former
- 3 mm, 4 mm and 8 mm beadmakers (CK)
- 15 cm/6 inch, 20 cm/8 inch and 25 cm/10 inch thin oval cake boards
- 43 cm/17 inch oval cake board
- Wood-graining tool
- 21 x 5 mm/¼ inch dowel rods
- Long sharpened dowel rod
- Lace wrap mould (ELI – 201)
- Lace cutter (FMM – M7)
- Lace rose mould (SB – 8F955)
- Scalloped-edged cutter (FMM – M7)
- Satay stick/bamboo skewer
- Textured fabric or ribbon, at least 2.5 cm/1 in wide
- Dressmaker's tracing wheel

INSPIRED BY A LOVE OF VICTORIAN ACCENTS, FLUID VINTAGE RIBBON ARRANGEMENTS DRAPE OVER GRACEFUL LACE. WHITE ON WHITE WITH ITS EXTENDED PALETTE OF NEUTRALS ARE NATURALS FOR A ROMANTIC FORMAL WEDDING. THIS CAKE DESIGN PAYS TRIBUTE TO PARISIAN FASHION DESIGNER CHRISTIAN LACROIX WHOSE MAGNIFICENT WORK INSPIRED ONE OF MY FAVOURITE WEDDING CAKES.

LISIANTHUS CENTRE

1 Using white flower paste/gum paste, make three small flat seed pods. Glue each to 28-gauge wire. Bind together with the floral tape. Brush with moss-green petal dust and colour the point with brown petal dust. For the stamens, mould five tiny rounded ovals with white paste. Glue each stamen to 28-gauge wire, then dampen slightly and dip into sifted fine polenta/cornmeal. Form a small fat sausage with green flower paste/gum paste. Push the taped seed pod wires into the top and through the sausage. Arrange the five stamens at equal distances around the sausage and position the pollen heads beneath the seed pods. Tape to the wires at the sausage base. Tape the whole lisianthus centre to an 18-gauge wire and continue taping to the stem base (pic 1).

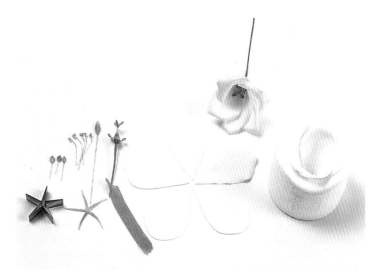

1 Making the lisianthus flowers

Roll up and place into a celformer that has been pierced through the base and dusted with cornflour/cornstarch. Separate the petals and prop with foam. Dust the merest hint of lime-green petal dust in the throat and at the flower tips. Push the wired stamens through the centre of the glued petals and secure with royal icing at the base. Check that the flower has not stuck to the former.

3 Cut the calyx from green paste, using the calyx cutter. Thin the sides with the ball tool, and pinch along the centre with tweezers. Glue in place beneath the petals.

THE TIARA

4 With the lace medallion cutter, prepare a lace-embossed, white flower paste/gum paste medallion. Brush with super pearl and then remove the eyelet holes. Cut the medallion base straight, using a craft knife (pic 2). Cover the rounded former with plain paper and lay the medallion on it until dry. Stand the piece up and

LISIANTHUS FLOWERS

2 Roll white flower paste/gum paste very thinly before cutting five petals, using the rose petal cutter or the lisianthus template (see page 155). If the rose petal cutter is used, slice the sides off the petals, as a lisianthus petal is much narrower than the rose. Although each petal can be wired, those shown here are not. Thin the petal edges with the ball tool and press into the palm of the hand to create veining. Glue the right side of each petal at the base for about one-third of its depth. Stack the petals into a fan, each overlapping by half. Furl the petals into a cone, checking that their bases are connected into a dull point.

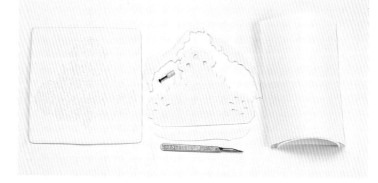

2 Tiara method from mould to former

embellish with three rows of stacked, graduated, 8 mm, 4 mm and 3 mm, white sugarpaste/rolled fondant beads (see beadmaking page 54). Brush with super pearl. Add two very thin single ribbons to tie at the back. For the finishing touch, attach two tiny four-looped bows at either side, covering the ribbon tapes. Add a single 4 mm bead at the centre of each bow.

STACKING THE CAKES

5 Centre the top three cake tiers on their matching-sized, thin cake boards, then cover each cake, including the bottom tier cake, with

3 Wood-grained cake board covering

white sugarpaste/rolled fondant. Cover the 43 cm/17 inch oval cake board with white paste and emboss it with the wood-graining tool (pic 3). Brush the embossed board with super pearl lustre dust, then centre the bottom cake on it. Dowel and stack the cakes (see page 142).

LACE WRAPS

6 Run the sugarpaste/rolled fondant through a pasta machine on setting three, or hand roll. Press into the lace wrap mould and rub with the palm of the hand. Turn the mould over; allow the paste to drop out by itself, then trim the scalloped edge with a craft knife or scalpel, and brush liberally with super pearl lustre dust (pic 4). Dampen the sides of the cake with a little boiled water. Once the lace-embossed paste has firmed, lay it face downwards on the lace wrap

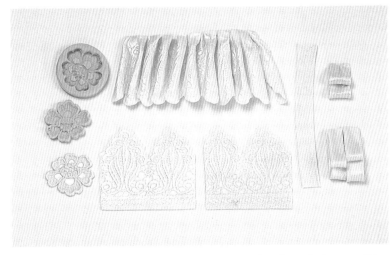

mould. Using the mould as support, attach one or two lengths of the lace-embossed paste to the side of each tier. Each wrap is 55 cm/22 inches long and goes right around the top tier, with a single join at the back. The second, third and bottom tiers each need two lace wraps. Seal the cakes with 8 mm sugarpaste/rolled fondant beads brushed with super pearl lustre dust.

4 Stages of the lace wrap, appliquéd flowers, bustle and vintage ribbons

This cake design would take centre stage at a typical American wedding. Made to be viewed from the front, back or side, it doesn't matter where it is placed at the event. Lisianthus or prairie gentians (*Eustoma grandiflorum*) are native to Texas, although the Japanese first popularized these long-lasting cut flowers. The pretty arc of each flower as it bends forward creates a soft and elegant silhouette.

DRAPES AND SWAGS

7 Measure and divide the bottom tier into four, finding the centre front and back, then the sides. Using these measurements, cut four panels of embossed lace in sugarpaste/rolled fondant, using a craft knife or scalpel. Embellish the edges with the lace cutter, then brush with super pearl lustre dust. Fold the top over and add an extra fold in the centre (pic 5). Attach each piece to the side of the bottom tier, draping from the centre front to the side, then side to back, back to side and finally side to front.

8 For the swags, measure the bottom tier cake on both front and back at mid-point between the centre front and centre back and the sides. Using these measurements, prepare the swags in the same way as the drapes. Make the appliquéd flowers by pressing sugarpaste/rolled fondant into the lace rose mould. Freeze the paste until the flower readily pops out of the mould. Leave to dry, brush with super pearl and attach each flower over a join on the cake board.

BUSTLE AND VINTAGE RIBBONS

9 Prepare a 50 x 9 cm/20 x 3¹/₂ inch panel of lace-embossed sugarpaste/rolled fondant, for the bustle. Trim the edge into scallops with the scalloped cutter and gather using a satay stick/bamboo skewer. Leave to firm, then attach to the cake back with a little boiled water.

10 To make the vintage ribbons, emboss thinly rolled sugarpaste/ rolled fondant with textured fabric or ribbon. Cut 2.5 cm/1 inch strips, fold the edges under, then fold in half. Vary the lengths so they balance the bustle. Layer these textured ribbons both front and back and on the sides. Prop with sponge foam, if the bustle begins to flatten.

5 Lace-edged drape and mould

FINISHING

11 For the back, make another sugarpaste/rolled fondant flounce of embossed lace, measuring 50 x 6 cm/20 x 2¹/₂ inches, and gather so it fits the space over the top of the ribbons. Pleat a neat little lace-edged paste fan, dry it and then attach at the base of the third tier in the empty space behind the bustle and between the cake. Cover the join on the side ribbons with two more appliquéd lace flowers. Using the same texturing medium, cut four 50 cm/20 inch paste ribbons and attach with a tiny amount of water to the cake side. Trim diagonally, then zip down the edge with the tracing wheel. Gently guide the ribbons to the centre front and attach with very little water. Add a 6 cm/2¹/₂ inch ball of white flower paste/gum

paste at the centre of the long ribbons. Hide the front and sides by extending the ribbon loops up and almost over, just leaving spaces for the lisianthus. Dry overnight. Attach the flowers, dipping each stem in royal icing and pushing it into the ball of flower paste/gum paste. Brush away any unattractive residue. Prop with sponge foam. (Back view of cake on page 149.)

AT THE RECEPTION

Add the top tier at the event site, then prepare and attach the pearl bead border. If only one person is available to carry this extremely heavy cake, it might also be worth adding the long ribbon loops on-site; then it would be necessary to carry only two tiers stacked. The tiara can be permanently attached into position with royal icing or be boxed and carried separately, to be retained as a souvenir.

And the Bride Chose Dogwood

Cake and Decoration

- 15 cm/6 inch, 20 cm/8 inch, 25 cm/10 inch and 30 cm/12 inch round cakes
- 15 g/$\frac{1}{2}$ oz mid-green flower paste/gum paste
- 250 g/8 oz ivory flower paste/gum paste
- Moss-green, pale yellow, lime and mushroom petal dusts (VB/CK)
- Silk-white lustre dust (VB/CK)
- Brown food colouring (VB/CK)
- 6 kg/12 lb ivory sugarpaste/rolled fondant
- Teacup mould for centrepiece base (see step 9)
- Champagne sugar crystals

Equipment

- Greased tulle netting
- 24-gauge wire
- Medium rose cutter (OP – R2, or similar)
- Paper templates of elongated petal and dogwood leaf (see page 157)
- Small blossom cutter
- Veining tool
- Aluminium foil
- Round piping tube/tip (W – 110)
- Fine tweezers
- 15 cm/6 inch, 20 cm/8 inch, 25 cm/10 inch thin round cake boards
- 35 cm/14 inch round cake board
- Ivory ribbon, 1.5 cm/$\frac{5}{8}$ inches wide, to trim the 35 cm/14 inch cake board
- Grosgrain-textured rolling pin (EC)
- Turntable (optional)
- Sponge foam
- 7 x 1 cm/$\frac{1}{2}$ inch dowel rods
- 12 x 5 mm/$\frac{1}{4}$ inch dowel rods

SAVING THE BEST FOR LAST! GLOWING WITH SUBTLE MOTHER-OF-PEARL SHEEN, DELICATE TRACERIES OF DOGWOODS ENCIRCLE THIS ELEGANT WEDDING CAKE, ILLUSTRATING SKILFULLY BLENDED, CLASSIC DESIGN AND CONTEMPORARY OVERTONES. ANOTHER SPECIAL SUGAR-ART TOUCH: THE FOOTED VASE WITH ITS SIMPLE CLUSTER OF MATCHING FLOWERS.

DOGWOOD FLOWERS

1 For the centre, press a pea-sized ball of mid-green flower paste/gum paste into the piece of greased tulle netting. Remove and check the shape is round. Gum glue miniscule ivory flower paste/gum paste cones on top of the centre, to suggest buds and florets. Make and wire seven such flower centres, and set aside to dry. Paint with clear alcohol/vodka or Everclear mixed with moss-green and pale yellow petal dusts.

2 Cut a pair of ivory flower paste/gum paste petals using the medium rose cutter or similar (two options are shown in pic 1), then cut another pair using the elongated petal template. Remove a small U-shape from the tops of both pairs, using the side of the small blossom cutter.

3 Thin the petal edges, then deeply vein with long strokes from top to base of each petal. Push the veining tool point into each cutout, so creating a slight hump across the petal tip. Lay the first pair of petals on a piece of shaped aluminium foil and gum glue together, then attach the elongated pair, forming a crucifix. Glue the flower centre over the join. Set aside to dry. Highlight the petals with lime petal dust, then silk-white lustre dust. Paint the cutouts with brown food colouring diluted with clear alcohol/vodka or Everclear. When thoroughly dry, dust the cutouts with mushroom petal dust. Make forty unwired flowers.

TO DRY WIRED FLOWERS

Push the wire on each flower through a hole in some shaped aluminium foil positioned over a tall drinking glass, resting the flower head on the foil. Leave until thoroughly dry.

DOGWOOD STEMS

4 Form a slim roll of ivory flower paste/gum paste and thread on to each wire. Bend in the desired stem shape, before drying. Brush with moss-green and lime petal dusts. Make small paste leaves freehand, and attach to the stems.

DOGWOOD FOLIAGE

5 For the side design, real dogwood leaves were used (see page 157 for the paper templates). Using the template or a commercial leaf cutter, cut out ivory flower paste/gum paste leaves, vein, brush with silk-white lustre dust and highlight with lime petal dust. Prepare about ninety leaves.

DOGWOOD SEED PODS

6 Prepare small cones freehand from ivory flower paste/gum paste. Impress the top with the piping tube/tip, and form ridges with fine tweezers. Brush with silk-white lustre dust, then lime and mushroom petal dusts. Dry.

GROSGRAIN RIBBON

7 Cover the cakes and boards with ivory sugarpaste/rolled fondant. Attach the ribbon to the board edge.

8 Emboss ivory sugarpaste/rolled fondant with the grosgrain-textured rolling pin. Measure the base of each cake, cut the embossed paste in appropriate, single lengths, and allow to firm up for a few minutes. Attach a strip to each cake, using a turntable if available, or placing the cake

1 Stages of the dogwood flowers and leaves

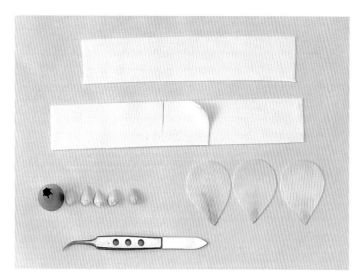

2 Grosgrain-textured dogwood blossoms

FINISHING

11 Stack the cakes using dowel support (see page 142). Attach the dogwood flowers, foliage and seed pods to the cake sides, with royal icing; particularly check each flower before moving on to the next. If nervous, prop the flowers with pieces of sponge foam until the royal icing is dry. The foliage and seed pods are much lighter and not likely to fall off while the royal icing is still wet.

12 Scatter and attach several leaves and seed pods on the paste-covered cake board. The day before moving the cake to the reception site, position the floral centrepiece centrally on the top cake, and secure with royal icing. (If the centrepiece is required as a family memento, pack separately and position on the cake on-site.)

board on a slippery surface and turning it by hand; start at the back and allow the paste ribbon to wrap itself round the cake. Cut overlapping ribbons for a perfect join and seal with royal icing. Remove the excess pieces of paste.

CENTREPIECE BASE

9 Create an ivory moulded sugar vase (see pages 74–5), using a prettily shaped teacup. Gouge out the centre with a teaspoon and dry thoroughly. Fill the centre with a ball of stiff sugarpaste/rolled fondant, flattened on the surface. Sprinkle with the sugar crystals and dry for a day. Emboss ivory flower paste/gum paste with the grosgrain-textured rolling pin and cut out single dogwood petals (pic 2). Attach to the outer surface of the moulded sugar vase. Cover the join of the sugar base with a thin strip of embossed, ivory flower paste/gum paste; then add miniature rolls of paste dusted pale lime.

10 Dip the stems of the wired flowers in thinned royal icing and push into the paste ball. Support in position with sponge foam until completely dry.

PRESENTATION

This cake can be set up on a table of honour, around which the guests can walk at the reception site. The design is continuous and since there is little difference from the front, back and sides there is no necessity for a special background.

PACKAGING

At the reception site, be sure to leave a strong cardboard box, written instructions for the staff, and the material for the cake top centrepiece to be repacked after the cake has been cut.

International Notes and Recipes

INGREDIENT VARIATIONS

• American butter is sold in pound packs. These are separated into 4 oz blocks known as sticks, each of which is marked on the side of the wrapper in 1 tbsp increments. One stick equals 4 oz, which is 115g; 1 tbsp equals 1/2 oz, which is 15g.

• Large eggs are used in all recipes in this book.

• American mills prepare plain flour/all-purpose flour from a combination of hard and soft wheat varieties, while UK mills use primarily soft wheat. British and Australian bakers preparing these recipes should therefore combine 50 per cent plain flour sifted together with 50 per cent strong bread flour.

• American 'Bakers' Special' (used professionally) or superfine sugar very closely resembles British and Australian caster sugar. Use any of these sugars in the recipes.

MEASURING INGREDIENTS

• American home bakers very rarely weigh ingredients, preferring to 'dip and sweep' with a measuring cup. When using a cup to measure flour, either spoon the flour into the cup or if the bin is wide and deep enough, dip the cup, then remove the excess by sweeping across the top of the cup with a flat spatula. Do not pack the flour down. There may be discrepancies with this method, because it is possible to repeat-weigh these dip-and-sweep ingredients six times and have six entirely differing results, some varying by as much as 55 g/2 oz. This is a major problem if you are expecting the perfect cake. By not using a set of scales, it is much easier to make a mistake in formulating the correct ratio of ingredients. Also cup and spoon measuring sets themselves can vary in capacity.

• The recipes in this book can be followed by using either metric or avoirdupois (imperial) measuring sets. Use only one set of measures.

• Finally, metric sets are slightly larger than imperial sets, so it follows that metric cake tins/pans should be used when using metric measurements and imperial cake tins/pans for imperial measuring sets.

ADJUSTMENTS FOR ALTITUDE

The recipes in this book were developed at sea level, so make alterations if you are baking at high altitude. Every 300 m/1,000 feet of altitude requires an additional adjustment. The most common changes to consider are:

• a reduction in bicarbonate of soda/baking soda or baking powder;
• a reduction in sugar;
• an increase in liquid weight. This can be accomplished with the addition of an egg white/yolk/or both;
• an increase in flour;
• an increase in oven temperature.

HEATING CONES

Prior to baking, fill the cake tin/pan to a smidgen over half full. To ensure even baking results in 8 cm/3 inch deep madeira/pound cakes, especially those of 30 cm/12 inch diameter or more, insert a heating cone. Grease the cone and lightly dust with flour both inside and out, position in the centre of the cake tin/pan, then half fill with the cake mixture/batter. After the cake has cooked and cooled, remove the heating cone. Turn out the cone-shaped cake, then return it to the space in the centre of the cake. Place the entire cake on a wire rack and allow to cool.

CAKE DECORATION ASSEMBLY TIMING

Directions for the assembly order in this book apply to Genoise, madeira/pound and sponge/white cakes, as these are perishable cakes and have to be made and decorated in a short time frame. Fruitcakes allow much more preparation time and can be made and decorated at whim.

CHOCOLATE

MELTING CHOCOLATE

There are many ways to melt dark or white chocolate and summer coat, from the inexpensive, familiar double boiler to the top-of-the-line Chocolate Sinsation. Something in between – the VIP Whistler – is a specialized pot that keeps chocolate or like products at an even temperature for dipping or pouring. Because the temperature of the Whistler is automatically controlled by the hydrothermic action of steam heat within the jacket lining, there is no burning or boiling over. It does not hold temper. At an average cost of £16/US$25, it is within the reach of most semi-professional and amateur sweet/candy makers.

WHITE CHOCOLATE

White chocolate as such really doesn't exist, as it does not contain any cocoa solids. However, you can buy two types of white colored chocolate: one contains cocoa butter as the only fat, and the other vegetable oil. Opt for a good brand such as Callebaut, Lindt, Nestlé, Tobler or Valrhona, all of which contain cocoa butter. Beware of inexpensive white chocolate – it will invariably be the inferior, vegetable oil variety. The shelf life of white chocolate is fairly limited, so be sure to use a retail source that sells it briskly. Use and eat immediately. Do not store for extended periods of time or, before you know it, it will have become quite rancid. Freezing is an option.

THE DOUBLE BOILER

Chocolate melts at 29°C/84°F. If using a double boiler, melt – don't cook – the chocolate over hot, not boiling, water. Take care: chocolate burns easily, so do not heat dark chocolate above 49°C/120°F or white above 43°C/110°F. Chocolate is often spoiled not only by overheating but also by steam contaminating the mixture, which makes the chocolate seize and so become almost useless, although it can still be piped. This will not happen with the VIP Whistler, as the steam is contained and the heat controlled.

THE MICROWAVE

The microwave can also be used to melt chocolate. Break the chocolate into small pieces and pile into a glass bowl. Melt uncovered with frequent bursts of low power (30 per cent), stirring frequently. The pieces will hold their shape and can trick one into overheating and burning the product.

RECIPES
SUGARPASTE/ROLLED FONDANT

Many sugarpaste/rolled fondant recipes are heavy to mix; this recipe shared by pastry chef Maria Velasquez of Texas is usable immediately and is not a strain to make.

INGREDIENTS
• 30 g/1 oz powdered gelatine
• 125 ml/4 fl oz/^{1}/$_2$ cup water
• 1 kg/2 lb sifted icing/confectioner's sugar
• 30 ml/1 oz/^{1}/$_4$ cup/2 tbsp glycerine
• 125 ml/4 oz/^{1}/$_2$ cup karo or light white corn syrup

Soften or bloom the gelatine in the water, then heat, but not to boiling point. Meanwhile warm the icing/confectioner's sugar in the oven at the lowest setting, then switch off (the sugar should only be body temperature). Add the glycerine and karo syrup to the warmed sugar. Combine both mixtures together. A heavy-duty machine on low speed using the dough hook can initially mix this. If the motor begins to strain, tip out on to the work surface, grease the hands with white vegetable shortening and finish manually. The mixture might look and feel a little lumpy but will smooth out during the kneading process.

COLOURING SUGARPASTE/ROLLED FONDANT

Always a laborious process, I find the easiest way to incorporate the colour with sugarpaste/rolled fondant is to dip a cocktail stick/toothpick into the chosen colour medium, which can be paste, liquid or powder – the last never seems to be as strong – and incorporate it into a small ball of paste. Knead a sufficient amount of colour into the ball until it reaches a shade several times deeper than required. Cut the ball in half and incorporate it into the paste. If the resultant mixture is too pale, add more from the remaining half ball until the desired shade is reached. Acting conservatively with colour is preferred, since once it is incorporated into the sugarpaste/rolled fondant, there is no way it can be reversed. Always wear food-approved gloves when using colouring paste, liquid or powder, to avoid colouring your hands and staining them semi-permanently.

ROYAL ICING
INGREDIENTS
• 1 egg white at room temperature (substitute with pasteurized/albumin powder, if necessary)
• 185–250 g/6–8 oz/1^1/$_2$–2 cups sifted icing/confectioner's sugar

Remove any embryonic tail from the egg white. Put the egg white in a glass bowl and break it up with a wooden spoon. Add the sugar 5 ml/1 tsp at a time, incorporating it thoroughly each time. Only once the egg white readily accepts the sugar can the amount of sugar added be increased. Hand mixing generally takes about 20 minutes.

• The quantity of sugar required depends on whether soft, medium or firm peak royal icing is preferred; use the lower amount for soft peak, more for firmer icing.

• When only small amounts of royal icing are required, make up a single recipe of royal icing, then divide it into generous 5 ml/1 tsp increments. Double wrap in plastic wrap, double bag, and place in the freezer until it is required.

FLOWER PASTE/GUM PASTE

INGREDIENTS

• 1 egg white at room temperature (or pasteurized/albumin powder)
• 185–250 g/6–8 oz/1½–2 cups sifted icing/confectioner's sugar
• 15 ml/3 tsp Tylose powder/CMC (J)
• 5–10 ml/1–2 tsp firm white vegetable shortening

Proceed as for royal icing until the sugar reaches soft peak stage, then add the Tylose powder. Even though the mixture will immediately seize, continue adding sugar until the mixture is no longer sticky. Warm the shortening in the palms of the hands, then knead it into the mixture. Double wrap the paste tightly in plastic wrap and store in the refrigerator or freezer.

PASTILLAGE

INGREDIENTS

• 500 g/1 lb/4 cups icing/confectioner's sugar
• 15 ml/1 tbsp gum tragacanth
• 60 ml/2 fl oz/¼ cup water

Grease the bowl, paddle/beater and hands. On a slow setting, mix all the ingredients together, except for about ⅔ cup sugar. Grease the work surface/countertop, pour on the rest of the sugar and knead into the mixture.

The pastillage can be used immediately. However, it will dry out a faster than flower paste/gum paste so don't use it for anything that takes a long time to make.

DECORATOR'S BUTTERCREAM

This recipe makes sufficient to ice/frost and decorate a 25 cm/10 inch round cake or 23 x 33 cm/9 x 13 inch rectangular/sheet cake.

INGREDIENTS

• 25 ml/5 tsp meringue powder (substitute with 15 ml/3 tsp albumin powder, if necessary)
• 1.5 kg /3 lb icing/confectioner's sugar
• 2.5 ml/½ tsp cream of tartar
• 250 g/8 oz/1 cup unsalted/sweet butter and firm white vegetable shortening in a 50:50 mix (or 25:75 in hot temperatures)
• 185 ml/6 fl oz/¾ cup water
• 15 ml/1 tbsp pure vanilla (substitute with white imitation, if necessary)

1 Sift the dry ingredients in a large mixing bowl. Add the rest, blending well at low speed in an electric stand mixer, then beat at high speed for 5 minutes.
2 For icing/frosting the cake, mix in more fluid. For piped decorations, add a little more sugar.

ITALIAN MERINGUE BUTTERCREAM

This is sufficient to ice/frost a 20 cm/8 inch, double-layered cake.

INGREDIENTS

• 6 large egg whites
• 440 g/14 oz/1¾ cups caster/superfine sugar
• 1.25 ml/¼ tsp cream of tartar
• 500 g/1 lb/4 sticks unsalted butter/sweet butter at room temperature
• 15 ml/1 tbsp vanilla essence/extract

1 Using an electric hand mixer, beat the egg whites over hot water in the top of a double boiler until soft peaks appear. Add the sugar and cream of tartar in small increments, beating continuously until a ribbon begins to form, when the mixture reaches 40°C/105°F.
2 Remove from the heat source and continue beating until the mixture cools to room temperature. This may take 20 minutes or so.
3 Chop the butter in small pieces and introduce gradually. Increase the size of the pieces once half of the butter is incorporated into the mixture. Add the vanilla gradually.

CITRON VODKA CAKE

This cake is extremely rich, very delicious and not for anyone watching their calories.

Makes a 25 cm/10 inch round cake, 8 cm/ 3 inches deep.

CAKE INGREDIENTS

• 250 g/8 oz/2 sticks butter, softened
• 440 g/14 oz/1¾ cups caster/superfine sugar
• 5 ml/1 tsp vanilla essence/extract
• 4 large eggs
• 600 g/1¼ lb/5 cups plain flour/all-purpose flour
• 5 ml/1 tsp salt
• 5 ml/1 tsp baking powder

- 2.5 ml/^{1}/$_2$ tsp bicarbonate of
  soda/baking soda
- 250 ml/8 fl oz/1 cup buttermilk
- 10 ml/2 tsp lemon essence/extract
- 60 ml/2 fl oz/^{1}/$_4$ cup lemon juice
- Zest of two large lemons

SAUCE INGREDIENTS
- 250 g/8 oz/1 cup caster/superfine sugar
- 125 g/4 oz/1 stick butter
- 10 ml/2 tsp lemon essence/extract
- Juice of one lemon, made up to
  125 ml/4 fl oz/^{1}/$_2$ cup with
  Stolichnaya Citron (Lemon)
  Vodka. Do not substitute.

1 Grease a 25 cm/10 inch round cake
tin/pan, 8 cm/ 3 inch deep. Preheat the
oven to 170°C/325°F/GM3. Cream the
butter and sugar until light and fluffy.
Add the vanilla, then the eggs, one at a
time. Sift the dry ingredients and add
alternately with the buttermilk and
lemon essence, starting and ending with
flour. Mix for 2 minutes at medium
speed. Add the lemon juice and zest.
2 Fill the cake tin/pan, put in the
preheated oven and bake for 60–65
minutes. (If the mixture has been divided
between two shallower, 25 cm/ 10 inch
tins/pans, check earlier, after about 45
minutes.) Test with a skewer before
removing from the oven.
3 Meanwhile, about 10 minutes before
the cake is ready to come out of the oven,
mix the ingredients for the lemon vodka
sauce. Heat the ingredients together, just
enough to melt the butter. Do not allow
the mixture to boil. Immediately prick
the cake all over with a satay
stick/bamboo skewer and pour the lemon
vodka sauce over the hot cake. This will
not hurt the cake as the holes will fill
with the sauce and the cake crumb will

absorb the liquid and begin to swell. Do
not remove it from the tin/pan until it
is properly cold.

ITALIAN CREAM CAKE

This is an excellent alternative to a
fruitcake for a wedding, and it can be
made at least five days ahead.

Makes two 25 cm/10 inch round cakes,
5 cm/2 inches deep.

INGREDIENTS
- 125 ml/4 fl oz/^{1}/$_2$ cup vegetable oil
- 125 g/4 oz/1 stick unsalted butter/
  sweet butter
- 500 g/1 lb/2 cups caster/superfine
  sugar
- 5 ml/1 tsp vanilla essence/extract
- 5 large eggs, separated
- 5 ml/1 tsp bicarbonate of soda/
  baking soda
- 250 ml/8 fl oz/1 cup buttermilk
- 1.25 ml/^{1}/$_4$ tsp salt
- 250 g/8 oz/2 cups plain flour/
  all-purpose flour
- 125 g/4 oz/1 cup chopped pecans
- 65 g/2^1/$_4$ oz/1 cup flake coconut
  (frozen is best if you can get it,
  otherwise use moist dried)

1 Lightly grease two 25 cm/10 inch
round cake tins/pans, 5 cm/2 inches
deep with margarine, then dust with
flour. Alternatively, prepare the tins/pans
using a commercial spray or paint them
with a whipped mixture of equal parts
vegetable oil, plain flour/all-purpose
flour and vegetable fat. Set the oven at
180°C/350°F/GM4.
2 Mix the oil and butter, then add the
sugar, and cream well. Add the vanilla,
and then the egg yolks one at a time
until the mixture is light and fluffy
but not curdled. Combine the

bicarbonate of soda/baking soda with
the buttermilk. Add salt to the cake
mixture/batter, then sifted flour
alternately with the buttermilk. Finally
stir in the pecans and coconut. Beat the
egg whites until stiff, and fold into the
mix in three batches.
3 Fill the cake tins/pans and bake in the
preheated oven for 40–50 minutes,
depending on the oven. Check with a
cake tester. This cake will be very moist,
providing plenty of time to decorate.

If this recipe has been baked in a
25 cm/10 inch round cake tin/pan, 8 cm/
3 inches deep, drop the oven temperature
by 10°C/50°F. To keep the surface of this
heavier-textured cake from drying out,
create steam by adding a small pan of
water in the lower part of the oven.

ROSELLA GINGER
PECAN TORTE

This cake was a national finalist in a
wedding cake competition held in the
United States. It can be made and
assembled five days before a wedding. In
fact, the maturing process improves the
combination of flavours. This recipe can
be made 'as is' or mix and match to suit.

Makes two 25 cm/10 inch round cakes.
Reduce them by a third for two 20 cm/8
inch round cakes.

CAKE INGREDIENTS
- 125 g/4 oz fresh pineapple (or drained
  crushed pineapple, if necessary)
- 360 g/12 oz ripe Anjou pears
  (or well-drained canned pears, if
  necessary)
- 440 g/14 oz/1^3/$_4$ cups caster/
  superfine sugar
- One lemon, sliced
- Stick lemon grass/lemon serai
  (optional)

- 410 g/13 oz/3$\frac{1}{2}$ cups plain flour/all-purpose flour
- 5 ml/1 tsp salt
- 15 ml/1 tbsp baking powder
- 23 ml/1$\frac{1}{2}$ tbsp powdered ginger
- 250 g/8 oz/2 sticks butter
- 15 ml/1 tbsp Madagascar bourbon vanilla essence/extract (NM)
- 125 g/4 oz/$\frac{1}{2}$ cup brown sugar
- 4 large eggs
- 80 ml/3$\frac{1}{2}$ oz/$\frac{1}{2}$ cup oil
- 30 ml/2 tbsp golden syrup/golden cane syrup
- 250 g/8 oz/2 cups toasted pecans, finely chopped (Wichita's and Elliott)
- 60 g/2 oz/$\frac{3}{4}$ cup fresh grated coconut (substitute with desiccated coconut, if necessary)
- 125 g/4 oz/$\frac{1}{2}$ cup glacé baby ginger, chopped small (B)

SYRUP INGREDIENTS
- 45 ml/3 tbsp sugar
- 90 ml/6 tbsp water
- 120 ml/8 tbsp ginger wine (S)

1 Steam, drain and chop the pineapple in the food processor. Poach the pears, adding 45 ml/3 tbsp of the sugar, lemon slices and lemon grass/lemon serai to the steaming water. Grate the pears, then drain and press for one hour before using. Grease, flour and parchment-line two 25 cm/10 inch cake tins/pan. Preheat the oven to 180°C/350°F/GM4.

2 Sift together the flour, salt, baking powder and ginger, and set aside. Beat the butter, vanilla and remaining sugar until light and fluffy. Add eggs one at a time, beating well between each addition. Add the sifted ingredients, then the oil and syrup. Mix for 2 minutes on medium speed – this gives time to activate the flour then fold in the nuts and ginger.

3 Pour the mixture/batter into the prepared cake tins/pans and bake for 45 minutes, but check after 30 minutes, in case your oven is not properly calibrated. Cool for 20 minutes, then turn on to a cooling rack and pour over the ginger syrup. (I used a hypodermic to distribute the syrup evenly.)

4 To make the ginger syrup, simmer the sugar in the water until it dissolves entirely. Cool completely, then add the ginger wine.

MERINGUE DACQUOISE
- 6 large egg whites
- 250 g/8 oz/2 cups icing/confectioner's sugar, sifted
- 250 g/8 oz/2 cups toasted pecans, coarsely ground
- 23 ml/1$\frac{1}{2}$ tbsp plain flour/all-purpose flour, sifted
- 23 ml/1$\frac{1}{2}$ tbsp potato flour, sifted
- 8 ml/1$\frac{1}{2}$ tsp sifted Madagascar bourbon vanilla powder (NM) (or 5 ml/1 tsp vanilla essence extract)
- 8 ml/1$\frac{1}{2}$ tsp good-quality cocoa (Droste or Guittard), sifted

5 For the meringue, first preheat the oven to 180°C/350°F/GM4. Draw two 25 cm/10 inch circles on parchment, and place on an oven tray. Whip the egg whites until they are stiff but not dry. Add the sugar in three stages, mixing well between each addition. Then, add the nuts. Sift together the two flours, powdered vanilla and cocoa, then add to the mixture, folding in the flours and powders carefully with a light hand. (For competition, sift and add separately.) Spoon the mixture into the circles, level and bake in the preheated oven for 20 minutes, or until they have turned a pale golden brown.

STRAINED GINGER MARMALADE
- 300 g/10 oz jar baby ginger marmalade (B)
- 30 ml/2 tbsp lemon juice
- 45 ml/3 tbsp water
- 30 ml/2 tbsp butter
- 45 ml/3 tbsp ginger wine (S)

6 Heat the ginger marmalade, lemon juice, water and butter gently in a double boiler. Purée in the food processor, strain. When cool add the ginger wine.

GINGER AND CHOCOLATE GANACHE
- 300 g/10 oz plain bitter/bittersweet chocolate
- 315 ml/10 fl oz/1$\frac{1}{4}$ cups double cream/heavy cream
- 55 g/2 oz baby ginger, finely chopped (B)
- 85 g/3 oz/$\frac{3}{4}$ cup toasted pecans, finely chopped
- 45 ml/3 tbsp ginger wine (S)

7 Melt the chocolate over hot, not boiling, water. Add the cream, ginger and pecans. After cooling, add the ginger wine. Stir well and allow to thicken.

MY MOTHER'S WASHED CREAM
- 250 g/8 oz/1 cup unsalted/sweet butter
- 15 ml/1 tbsp Madagascar bourbon vanilla essence/extract (NM)
- 30 ml/2 tbsp uncooked honey
- 100 g/3$\frac{1}{2}$ oz/$\frac{1}{2}$ cup caster/superfine sugar

8 For the cream, whip all ingredients until light and fluffy. Remove the bowl from the mixer. Cover with chilled water, swirl and squeeze through the fingers for a minute, drain the water thoroughly and re-beat

until light and fluffy. Repeat six times until white and the sugar is totally dissolved. Keep covered in a cool place, without refrigeration, or stored tightly covered in the refrigerator for up to a month.

ASSEMBLY

9 Level the cakes if necessary (see page 140). Secure greaseproof/wax paper to the cake board with royal icing. Place the meringue dacquoise on the greaseproof/wax paper. Smooth a layer of washed cream, chocolate ganache and ginger marmalade on the meringue disc. Top with one of the cakes. Repeat the layers of washed cream, ganache and ginger marmalade with the second meringue disc. Top with washed cream, ganache and marmalade, then add the second cake. Trim the meringue discs. Coat the entire cake with washed cream, then the strained marmalade. Cover with plastic wrap for twenty-four hours. Chill. Cover with white chocolate sugarpaste/ rolled fondant.

WHITE CHOCOLATE SUGAR-PASTE/ROLLED FONDANT

For every 1 kg/2 lb sugarpaste/rolled fondant (see page 134), melt 250 g/8 oz either high-ratio cocoa butter white chocolate or chocolate couverture (compound). (If using couverture, add 85 g/ 3 oz/$\frac{1}{2}$ cup sifted Dutch-processed cocoa to the melted chocolate and knead well.) Pour the chocolate into the rested paste and knead until incorporated. If flaking occurs, microwave in 5 second increments until the paste warms. Leave overnight. This results in a soft and easy to manage sugarpaste/rolled fondant. Warm in the microwave for a few seconds before kneading. Roll out on sifted icing/confectioners' sugar or cocoa.

CAKE CUTTING CHARTS

The following cake-cutting directions are intended for madeira or sponge/pound or white cake. Triple the suggested numbers for fruitcake servings. Be reminded, wedding cake servings are not as large as those for dessert, and cake servers do not always cut exactly the same-sized slice. The chart is only as a general guide.

ROUND CAKES

DIAMETER	NO. PEOPLE SERVED
15 cm/6 inch	15
20 cm/8 inch	25
25 cm/10 inch	40
30 cm/12 inch	60
35 cm/14 inch	85
40 cm/16 inch	100
45 cm/18 inch	125

OVAL CAKES

SIZE	NO. PEOPLE SERVED
20 x 15 cm/8 x 6 inches	10
28 x 20 cm/11 x 8 inches	25
32 x 25 cm/13 x 10 inches	40
40 x 32 cm/16 x 13 inches	24

HEART-SHAPED CAKES

WIDTH	NO. PEOPLE SERVED
15 cm/6 inch	10
23 cm/9 inch	25
30 cm/12 inch	40
38 cm/15 inch	80

ALTERNATE WAYS TO CUT A ROUND CAKE

Method 1

Cut a circle 5 cm/2 inches in from the edge of the cake. Cut pieces approximately 2.5 cm/1 inch wide around that circle, with the knife pointing towards the centre of the cake all the time. Move in another 5 cm/2 inches, cut a circle and continue cutting and making further circles until the tier is served.

Method 2

Make a cut across the cake approximately 5 cm/2 inches from the edge. Slice off in approximately 2.5 cm/1 inch wide slices (end pieces will be a little larger because of the curve of the cake). Continue making cuts every 5 cm/2 inches and slicing in 2.5 cm/1 inch pieces until the tier is served.

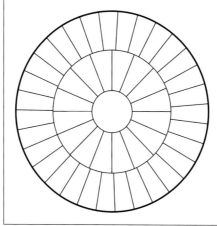
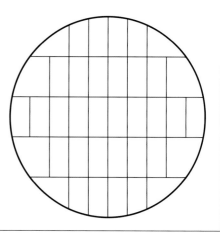

Bake it...Design it...Create it

COVERING A CAKE BOARD

Roll out the sugarpaste/rolled fondant to slightly larger than the cake board size. Slightly dampen the board and cover entirely with the paste. If liked, decorate with a textured rolling pin or crimper, depending on the pattern required (pic 2). Trim around the edge with a sharp knife, then smooth the rough edges with your hand or a set of smoothers. To disguise the raw edge to the board, attach a pretty ribbon or upholstery fabric, using fabric spray adhesive or a gum stick. For fruitcakes, an alternative method of covering a cake board is to roll out a strip of sugarpaste/rolled fondant and position it only between the cake and the board edge.

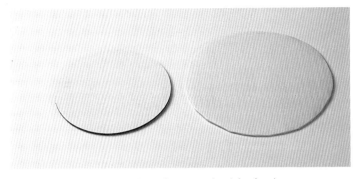

1 Thin American cake boards covered with plastic contact

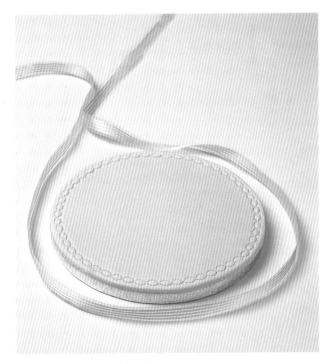

2 Covering a cake board

Thin foil cake boards usually need to be trimmed to size – the board must not be visible beyond the edge of the cake itself. In the United States, thin boards (pic 1) are not covered with protective foil so they have to be taken care of individually. Plastic contact shelf covering is the preferred method. Cut the size required in ivory or white, then peel off the paper backing and attach to the thin card board on both sides. This is especially necessary for sugarpaste/rolled fondant cakes, because of the passage of time needed to complete the design work. If not protected, the board might absorb moisture, then warp or buckle, and the cake could collapse.

AN ADDITIONAL NOTE FOR CAKE STYLISTS

Dry sugarpaste/rolled fondant-covered cake boards overnight before adding cakes larger than 30 cm/12 inches in diameter. If the paste is not dry, it is very hard to centre the cake and move it on the board without marring the surface. Position each madeira or sponge/pound or white cake on a thin cake board. Bring the paste right down over the cake board edge before centring and stacking on the main cake board. These cakes are fragile so handle them gently.

LEVELLING A CAKE

Freeze or chill the cake overnight to firm the crumb, then place it on a cake board. To level the cake top, either cut right across with a long knife (pic 3) or use a professional cake leveller (pic 4) – the latter being invaluable when dealing with a cake as large as 50 cm/20 inches diameter. Turn the cake over, so the bottom of the cake is now the top, and there will be fewer noticeable imperfections.

3 Levelling a cake by hand

4 Levelling a cake with a professional cake leveller

SCULPTING A CAKE

To sculpt a cake so its sides gradually incline inwards from the top, use a wide blade and cut down evenly, angling the knife inwards, until only a bare 1 cm/½ inch is removed at the base (pic 5). When doing this, err on the conservative side: the first time I attempted sculpting in this way, I chopped away large chunks and this was a mistake. Shaving the cake gradually is the correct way to proceed. Reception Confection cake (see page 86) has such sculpted sides.

To sculpt a 'waisted' cake, use a long, thin, very sharp knife to carve from the base up and the top down, creating a gradual inward curve and a shallow waist, 1 cm/½ inch deep. It doesn't take much cutting to achieve the 'waist' effect. (Also remember the more cake that is discarded, the fewer people it will serve, and this cost is passed on to the client.) The middle tier on All that Glitters cake (see page 52) is typical of this 'waisted' shape.

5 Sculpting a cake with sloping sides

6 Sculpting a 'waisted' cake

COVERING A CAKE

First, sandwich layered cakes with chosen filling. Paint the surface of the cake with a thin coat of seedless raspberry jam/jelly. Make no mistake: if this coating is lumpy the paste will not be forgiving. Remove any visible pieces of fruit by pulsing in a food processor, then sieving before use. Cover the cake with a thin layer of buttercream or the Italian meringue version (pic 7), then with sugarpaste/rolled fondant.

To cover a cake with sugarpaste/rolled fondant using lifters, brush the surface of the paste lifters with a very thin coating of white shortening, then wipe off the excess with a paper towel, and dust the surface with sifted cornflour/cornstarch. Roll out the sugarpaste/rolled fondant on the lifter's metallic surface, and trim away the excess. Lift the rolled paste over the cake (pic 8) and drop the lifter down over the cake board. You should have a perfect result every time. Smooth the surface with your hands or a commercial smoother, and trim away excess paste. I use a very large, thin, commercial scraper to cut away the excess from the edge of the cake (pic 9), and it can double up as a smoother. Polish the cakes with a ball of scrap sugarpaste/rolled fondant. Leave them to sit overnight before decorating.

7 Cake first covered with jam, then Italian buttercream

8 Sugarpaste/rolled fondant on a cake lifter

9 Trimming excess sugarpaste/rolled fondant

OTHER WAYS TO COVER A CAKE WITH SUGARPASTE/ROLLED FONDANT

Roll out the sugarpaste/rolled fondant roughly to the required size, and lift it over the cake with your hands or a rolling pin. This method becomes almost impossible as the cake size increases; when this happens, forget the rolling pin and lift the paste across both forearms, sharing the weight equally. Alternatively, roll out between two sheets of very thick plastic, peel away the top sheet, turn it over and lay over the cake before peeling away the other sheet.

DOWELLING A CAKE

Stacked cakes require the support of dowel rods to stop them collapsing. Currently I use wooden dowels to support my cakes; others prefer hollow plastic ones. However, some high-quality Stress-Free Cake Supports have recently become available (see Supplier's list, page 159), and these are so strong a person can stand on them. Each stainless-steel separator plate, in sizes ranging from 10 cm/4 inches to 40 cm/16 inches, will not warp and has four adjustable, nylon legs.

Whatever support material is used, the placement of the dowels is basically the same. Take the dowel measurement for each cake and cut to size. Evenly space in a circle and push into the cake with a finger (pic 10). Touch each dowel top with a blob of royal icing and, using an offset spatula, lift each cake into position. To avoid sliding or shifting problems when transporting or setting up the cake, especially with softly textured cake, hammer a long sharpened dowel, 5 mm/¼ inch thick, through the centre of the stacked cakes (pic 11). Mark where the dowel is even with the top of the cake, pull it out a little, clip it off with pruning shears kept especially for this purpose, and hammer it back down to its original position level with the top of the cake.

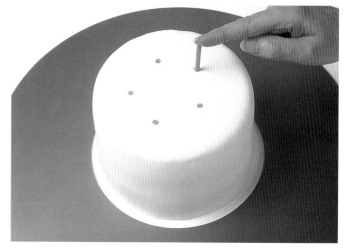

10 Inserting a short dowel

11 Inserting a long central dowel

Use 1 cm/½ inch dowel rods for the following cakes:
45 cm/18 inch cake – 11 dowels
40 cm/16 inch cake – 9 dowels
35 cm/14 inch cake – 9 dowels
30 cm/12 inch cake – 7 dowels

Use 5 mm/¼ inch dowel rods for the following cakes:
25 cm/10 inch cake – 7 dowels
20 cm/8 inch cake – 5 dowels
15 cm/6 inch cake – 5 dowels

For tiers second from top, use 2.5 mm/⅛ inch dowel rods. Dowels vary by cake. Heavier cakes require more substantial support. Each cake must be assessed on its own merit, according to the density of crumb.

AT THE RECEPTION

The dowels should be removed by the cake server. First remove the long central dowel, separate the cakes to serve, then remove the shorter ones as each cake is cut. Always indicate when a cake is dowelled.

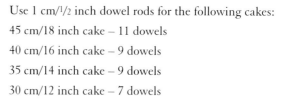

FABRIC-LIKE FLOURISHES

Because the main emphasis of this book has been focused on romance, there have been a variety of gathers, pleats, ruching and swag methods included. The following overview shows these techniques being hand applied.

GATHERS

Measure the depth of each cake. Roll out either flower paste/gum paste and sugarpaste/rolled fondant in a 50:50 mixture or just sugarpaste/rolled fondant alone, using a pasta machine if available. Cut out panels of the required size. Shorter, more manageable lengths will not compromise the design if long panels seem

1 Attaching gathers to the cake side

a bit daunting. Gather evenly, using satay sticks/bamboo skewers. While still soft, remove the sticks/skewers, press down firmly at the top and attach to the cakes with edible gum glue (pic 1). Hiding each join under the previous panel, continue overlapping panels until the last, which will slip under the first and so form a continuous skirt. Encourage the skirt to billow by teasing the edge out with a paintbrush. See also Picture Perfect Couture cake (page 35) for reference.

2 Using a pasta machine

ELECTRIC PASTA MACHINES

The pasta machine is especially useful for creating gathers, pleats, ruches, swags and flowers. It is a marvellous time-saver, too, and a must for anyone with carpal tunnel problems. Such a machine can be set at any thickness required for flower paste/gum paste or sugarpaste/rolled fondant, and it is also possible to produce extremely long strips of sugarpaste/rolled fondant without tearing (pic 2). However, if the same piece of sugarpaste/rolled fondant is fed through the machine more than three or four times, the stainless-steel rollers can affect the paste colour, giving it a grey tinge and making it overworked. The rubbery texture problem also occurs after repeatedly using a non-stick rolling pin on the same piece of paste, but there is no colour change.

PLEATS

Roll out the sugarpaste/rolled fondant by hand or with an electric pasta machine. With a craft knife or scalpel, cut the panels to the size required. Form into uniform-sized pleats with satay sticks/bamboo skewers (see pic 6, page 47). While still soft, remove the sticks and attach the pleated panels to the side of the cake with edible gum glue (pic 3). The last pleat will tuck under the first, so there will be no visible join. See also Romancing the Dome cake (page 44) for reference.

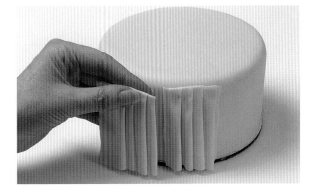

3 Attaching pleats to the cake side

RUCHING

Divide the cake evenly into 3 cm/1¼ inch sections. Roll out some sugarpaste/rolled fondant and cut it into 10 x 3 cm/4 x 1¼ inch panels. As each cake measurement differs, some adjustment may be necessary. After gathering (see page 143), press down hard to keep the ruched pleats together. Separate with a craft knife or scalpel. Attach the ruched panels to the side of the cake (pic 4) and cover the joins with strips of 5 mm/¼ inch paste using a lace edge cutter (FMM – M5). See also Glimpsed under Glass cake (page 91) for reference.

SWAGS

These are simple pre-measured panels of sugarpaste/rolled fondant divided with two or three folds. Measure and divide the cake into as many sections as required. After cutting the panels, use

4 Applying a ruched panel to the cake side

satay sticks/bamboo skewers or slim pieces of wood dowelling to separate and hold the folds in place evenly (see pic 6, page 47). While the paste is still soft, remove the sticks, pinch both ends together, and attach to the side of the cake with edible gum glue (pic 5). Cover the joins with decorative accents. See also Love is in the Air cake (page 120) for reference.

5 Attaching a swag to the cake side

6 Applying a rolled strip to the cake

CONTINUOUS ROLLED STRIPS FOR CONTINUOUS FOLDS

Run the sugarpaste/rolled fondant through the pasta machine and cut strips about 10 cm/4 inch wide by the circumference measurement of the cake. Trim the edges, fold each strip in half and attach to the cake with edible gum glue, starting at the top edge and progressing down the cake sides (pic 6). The strips can alternate in colour or remain solid, as in Simply Pretty in Pink (see page 116).

PINPRICKING THE SIDE DESIGN

TRANSFERRING THE PATTERN

1 Draw the side design on thin kitchen parchment or greaseproof/wax paper. (For quick repeat patterns, use parchment rather than paper in a photocopier.) Attach the paper pattern to the cake base with a pin at each side. Pinprick the design on to the cake side by pushing a pin repeatedly along the pattern outline (pic 1). Repeat the design, as necessary.

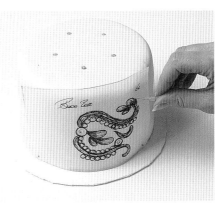

1 Pinpricking on to the cake

THE PASTE DECORATION

2 Place a copy of the pattern on the work surface/countertop and hand mould the scrolls, C-shapes and pearls. Check for the correct size and proportion by laying the prepared sugarpaste/rolled fondant pieces directly on to the pattern itself (pic 2). Paint the decorative pieces with the appropriate colours. (Here I have used super gold lustre dust mixed with clear alcohol/vodka or Everclear for the hand-moulded pieces, and super pearl lustre dust for the pearl accents).

3 Beginning with the largest pieces, attach the paste decoration to the cake side with edible gum glue. Correct any thinly painted spots with super gold lustre dust mixed with clear alcohol/vodka or Everclear (pic 3). (See All that Glitters on page 52.)

2 Checking the shape of the paste decoration

4 Hand mould the comma shapes, checking that they conform to the pattern. Paint in the same manner as in steps 2 and 3, and glue to the cake surface (pic 4). Fill in the base pattern with the pearl rope accents, pressing gently with the fingertips to ensure the gum glue makes direct contact with the cake surface (pic 5).

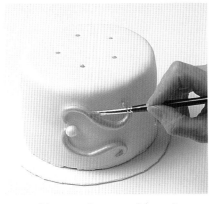

3 Touching up the paste decoration   *4 Building up the pattern*

EDIBLE GUM GLUE
To make edible gum glue, mix 15 g/½ oz sugarpaste/rolled fondant with enough water to dilute it into a thick syrupy mixture. Hurry it along with a couple of medium-temperature, 2 second bursts in the microwave. Store in the refrigerator in a capped container.

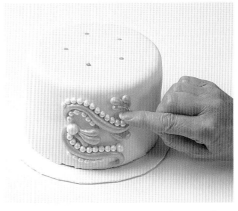

5 Attaching a pearl rope, pressing gently

A NEW SPIN ON CAKE PLATES

Scott Ferguson gave a demonstration on this technique, which I felt it was important to include here. An extremely classy cake plate or tray can be made for very little money and, if mislaid at a reception, is no one's loss.

EQUIPMENT

- Cake plate to be duplicated
- Foam core art board
- Clear craft spray
- Remnants of sugarpaste/rolled fondant or flower paste/gum paste
- Assorted moulds and textured rollers, such as smocking roller, fabric roller or a sheet of plastic cross-stitch canvas
- Edible gum glue
- Spray adhesive
- Plain florist's foil (without waterproof backing)
- Stiff brush, such as a basting or stencil brush
- Assorted sizes of ball tool
- Non-toxic artist's acrylic paint in colour of your choice
- Artist's brush

1 Embellishing the embossed board

PREPARING THE CAKE PLATE

1 Select a pattern to complement your cake, even using a cake tin/pan the same shape but a larger size than the cake itself. Allow at least a 5 cm/2 inch border around the cake. Duplicate the shape of the cake plate on the foam core board and cut out. Seal both sides with the clear craft spray, to help prevent warping.
2 Roll an even layer of flower paste/gum paste on to the board and emboss with a smocking roller, fabric roller or a sheet of plastic cross-stitch canvas. Embellish the embossed board with flower paste/gum paste, sugarpaste/rolled fondant or pastillage moulded in swags or lace wraps, secured with edible gum glue, or even royal icing piping (pic 1). Allow to dry thoroughly.

FOIL COVERING

3 Spray the entire top surface and edges with adhesive. Cut a piece of foil at least 5 cm/2 inch larger than the plate and gently lay over the embellished board, only pressing on to the adhesive when properly positioned. Starting from the centre and using a gentle, pouncing, circular motion, press the foil into the embossed paste with a stiff brush (pic 2). Gradually work your way towards the outside of the board, then over the edges and tuck under.
4 With a large ball tool, gently burnish the foil, working from the centre to the outside until every surface has been rubbed. Take a smaller ball tool and repeat the process. Use as many tools as you have and work down to a stylus-sized tool if you want a lot of detail. Cover the back with foil, if desired.
5 To dull the foil surface if it looks a bit too shiny and bright, apply an antique finishing solution of water-thinned acrylic paint

2 Stages of covering the embossed board with foil

over the entire surface; to simulate a natural patina, use a red-umber glaze on gold foil, black glaze on silver, dark brown or turquoise on copper. After application, immediately rub off the paint to reveal the moulded highlights (pic 3). This paint is non-toxic, but may be sealed if desired.

3 Completed plates with burnished finish

CAKE PLATES FOR HEAVY OR LARGE CAKES

If the cake is too large or heavy for a foam core art board, add a smaller commercial drum under the board 'plate' for support. Alternatively, cut the plate shape from hardboard or plywood.

SHIPPING CAKES

Is it possible to have a cake shipped across country? Yes. Will it arrive damage free? Maybe, but not necessarily and one definitely can't guarantee. You can't get the design of a cake you have seen by a particular cake stylist out of your head? Research then reveals their premises is 1000 miles away, so the shipping option comes immediately to mind.

Although it is possible to have a cake shipped long distance damage free, I would suggest that you first try to find someone in your own area to duplicate the design – or even improve on it. Give the local cake designer some artistic flexibility; most really don't want to reproduce exact copies.

If you reject the local option, look for a door-to-door courier that provides a pickup and delivery service. The price is likely to be hefty, starting from £200/US$300 for a three-tiered cake, and variables will depend on destination and weight.

Shipped cakes should always include detailed instructions for assembling the cake at the reception site. Even insuring a cake in transit, however, does not guarantee that you will have a cake at the reception. Each tier should be wrapped separately. Packing may or may not include dry ice, depending on the type of cake and the time of year. Fruitcake would not require ice; however, it is a must for chocolate couverture, buttercream icings, and madeira/pound cakes with tender fillings, especially when outside temperatures are above 15°C/59°F.

All decorative designs for the cake should be chosen with shipping in mind. Commercial flower paste/gum paste flowers are less likely to break than the finest handmade flower paste/gum paste flowers, as they are much thicker and more robust. Plaques, moulded flowers and close-to-the-surface, decorative work are also more likely to survive. If an accident happens, the responsibility lies with the baker unless the client signs a waiver. Having been a guest at several weddings where the cake was shipped in and damage was very noticeable, I later questioned the baker about responsibility and the airy reply was 'oh the resident chef will always fix it'. In my opinion, it is not the resident chef's business; he is not being paid to fix anything, since the cake was commissioned outside the establishment. On each occasion, no-one had put in a call to the chef to say that a cake was arriving by air and, should minimal damage occur in transit, would they consider patching it up as a professional courtesy. Even if the cake stylist arranges for a local baker to be available to assemble the cake and correct damage at the reception site, this might still not result in a top-quality cake. Respected bakers will already be involved with their own creations and deliveries, and it would be most embarrassing for their company profile to be seen dealing with another's mistakes. I feel similarly: I would not want to be anywhere near a disaster, as it would be a direct reflection on my business.

Fortunately, some companies provide transport and are willing to send a driver and the cake to distant parts. This is usually satisfactory, as the driver will assemble the cake on arrival, then repair damage if necessary. The charge is assessed on mileage and an hourly rate for the driver, and can quickly escalate to around £380/US$500.

Romantic Table Trends

GUEST DESIGNS BY DONNA DAVIS

THE UNDER-SKIRT

Under-skirting is usually a straight piece of fabric slightly shorter than the height of the display table. Polyester double-knit is a good choice, since the cut edge will not unravel; however, any fabric of the desired colour may be used. The colour may match the over-skirt or may complement the colour used on the cake.

THE OVER-SKIRT

Over-skirting may be assembled as one piece, long enough to go around the table, or in 1.2 m/4 feet lengths, depending on the type of fabric chosen. The latter may allow for easier cleaning after use – if just one panel is stained, it can be laundered independently.

AMERICAN WEDDINGS ARE STAGED PRODUCTIONS WITH A HINT OF THEATRE. FULL-SIZED, FABRIC-DRAPED CANOPIES, LATTICE GAZEBOS AND ENTIRE CEILINGS DECORATED WITH GREENERY AND TWINKLING MINIATURE LIGHTS PROVIDE THE PERFECT BACKDROP FOR THE CAKE.

Great thought is given to table linen and floral centrepieces. Backs of slip-covered chairs are matched with elaborate bows and flowers. Most often, these accessories are custom made just for the day. The table of honour is always lavishly decorated with fresh flowers and beautiful linen. It is the main focus of attention after the bride. Generally set up in the foyer or in the middle of the function room, the cake is seen from all angles.

TABLE 1

PREPARING THE OVER-SKIRT

1 To drape a table with material such as this heavily embroidered, pearl-beaded, double-edged, scalloped fabric, you will need one and one half times the circumference of the table. Measure the distance from the top of your chosen table to the floor, and add 2.5 cm/1 inch. Measure up this amount from the heavily decorated edge of the fabric. Trim the excess material from the lightest embroidery edge, then turn the trimmed edge so the right sides of both pieces are facing up. Place cut edges together. Turn under 5 mm/^{1}/4 inch towards the wrong side of the fabric and press. Turn under an additional 2 cm/^{3}/4 inch and press. This will make the casing to run a drapery drawstring through. Sew two lines of stitching, one at the bottom edge of the casing, and one near the top edge, which will make a small ruffle at the top of the skirting. Insert the drawstring. This will make a full-length drape with a short ruffle accent at the top.

PREPARING THE TRIM

2 To accent this table, use a 10 cm/4 inch wide bias polyester satin trim (see Making a continuous bias strip on page 150). For a tailored look, the ends of the trim may be hidden behind the table or, for a Victorian look, they may be arranged in any manner you wish, such as bows or streamers.

DRAPING THE TABLE

3 Cover the top of the table with a cloth either in a colour that matches the over-skirt or in a contrasting one. Pin the straight under-skirt to the tablecloth with pearl-headed corsage pins or straight pins, inserting them vertically into the material. (It is helpful at this stage to put something heavy on the tabletop to keep the fabric from shifting.) Gather the over-skirt to fit around the table and pin it on with pearl-headed corsage pins (pic 1). Pin the bias trim to the edge of the

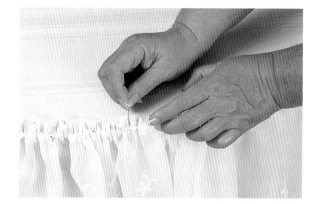

1 Attaching the over-skirt

tabletop, placing the seam edge of the bias strip next to the gathered edge of the over-skirt, with the outside of the bias strip on the tabletop (pic 2). Pin to the tablecloth, each pin very close to the next. Every 30 cm/12 inches or so, turn the

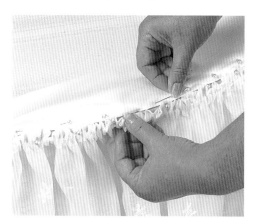

2 Attaching the bias trim

bias trim over the edge of the table to be sure the pinning is not too tight or too loose. When completed, fold the trim over the gathered edge of the over-skirt. On this table, the ends of the bias strip have been allowed to hang as streamers, off-centre to the side of the table. To create a decorative accent to the table, add a corsage of fresh roses and ivy.

MAKING A CONTINUOUS BIAS STRIP

Cut a square of fabric, using the width of your chosen material to determine the size. Fold the square diagonally (along dotted line in diagram, right); cut on this diagonal line. Sew section A to the far side of section B, making a parallelogram.

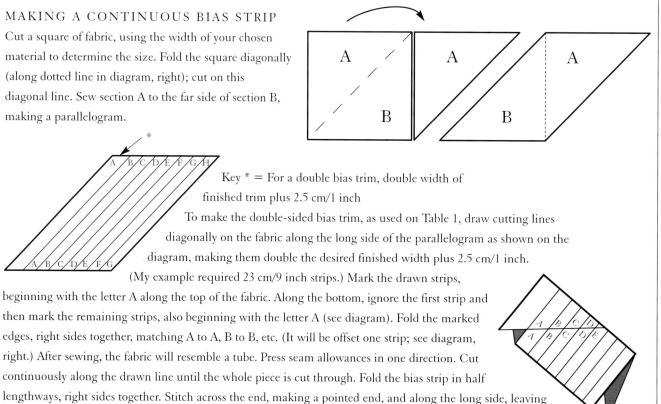

Key * = For a double bias trim, double width of finished trim plus 2.5 cm/1 inch

To make the double-sided bias trim, as used on Table 1, draw cutting lines diagonally on the fabric along the long side of the parallelogram as shown on the diagram, making them double the desired finished width plus 2.5 cm/1 inch. (My example required 23 cm/9 inch strips.) Mark the drawn strips, beginning with the letter A along the top of the fabric. Along the bottom, ignore the first strip and then mark the remaining strips, also beginning with the letter A (see diagram). Fold the marked edges, right sides together, matching A to A, B to B, etc. (It will be offset one strip; see diagram, right.) After sewing, the fabric will resemble a tube. Press seam allowances in one direction. Cut continuously along the drawn line until the whole piece is cut through. Fold the bias strip in half lengthways, right sides together. Stitch across the end, making a pointed end, and along the long side, leaving an opening in the centre of the strip, to allow for turning. Turn, press and handstitch the open portion.

TABLE 2
PREPARING THE OVER-SKIRT

1 This over-skirting is made of georgette, a very soft, flowing material with a drawstring top and a deep hem. Measure the distance from the floor to the tabletop. Turn under 2 cm/³/4 inch on the selvage edge and stitch as for Table 1, to make the casing. If a larger ruffle is desired at the top of the table, increase the amount turned under. Measure from the top stitching line down to the desired finished length of the drape. Turn up the balance of the fabric to make a wide hem, then stitch.

3 Attaching the under-skirt

PREPARING THE TRIM

2 This table has a double trim. The first is an all-over, heavily embroidered fabric with a scalloped edge on each selvage. Cut the fabric in half lengthways and seam to make one long piece. For the drawstring casing, turn under a very narrow hem plus 1 cm/¹/2 inch and stitch, leaving a long drop from the top of the table. Insert the drawstring. Make the second trim from the georgette – to measure three-quarters of the table's circumference. Cut this piece in half lengthways and seam together to make a swag one and a half times the table's circumference.

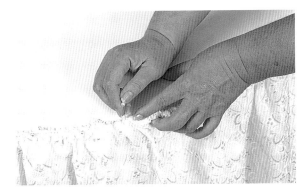

4 Attaching the first trim

DRAPING THE TABLE

3 Cover the tabletop, then add the under-skirt (pic 3) and over-skirt, as described for Table 1. Gather the first trim and attach with pearl-headed corsage pins (pic 4). Fold the swag in half lengthways to find the centre. Place this at the centre front of the table and gather at even intervals, pinning to make the swags (pic 5). Add fresh or silk flowers and ivy to each point of the swag.

5 Pinning the swag and flowers

Templates

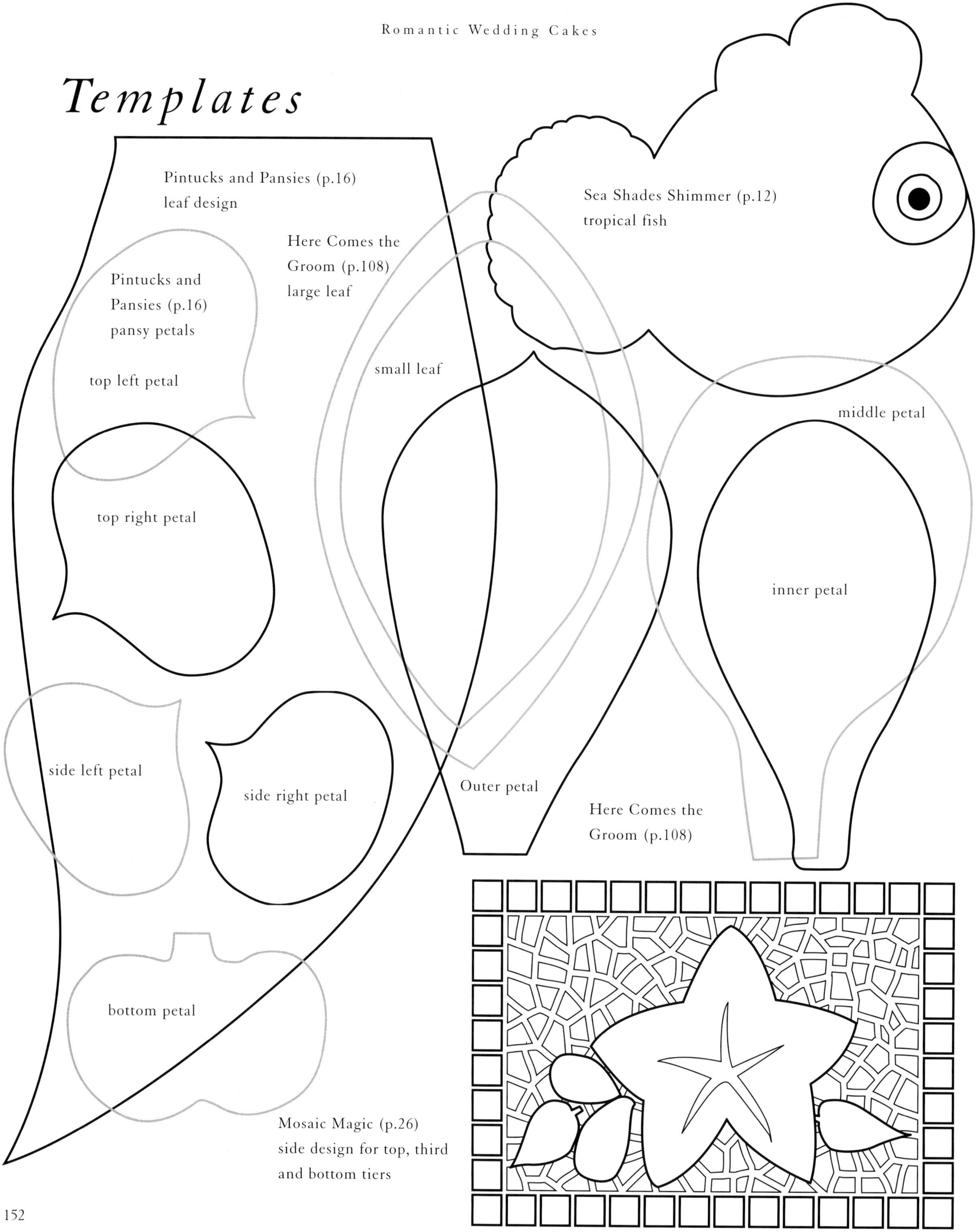

Pintucks and Pansies (p.16)
leaf design

Sea Shades Shimmer (p.12)
tropical fish

Pintucks and
Pansies (p.16)
pansy petals

top left petal

Here Comes the
Groom (p.108)
large leaf

small leaf

middle petal

top right petal

inner petal

side left petal

side right petal

Outer petal

Here Comes the
Groom (p.108)

bottom petal

Mosaic Magic (p.26)
side design for top, third
and bottom tiers

Mosaic Magic (p.26)
hydrangea flower –
medium petals

Mosaic Magic (p.26)
side design for second
and fourth tiers

side design for
bottom tier

side design for
top tier

Tiers in a Teacup (p.48)

Mosaic Magic (p.26)
star-shaped balloon
flower

Mosaic Magic (p.26)
hydrangea flower – large
and small petals

Valentine's Heart Sublime (p.40)
four-pointed gardenia leaf

All That Glitters (p.52)
side design for bottom tier

All That Glitters
(p.52)
side design for
top tier

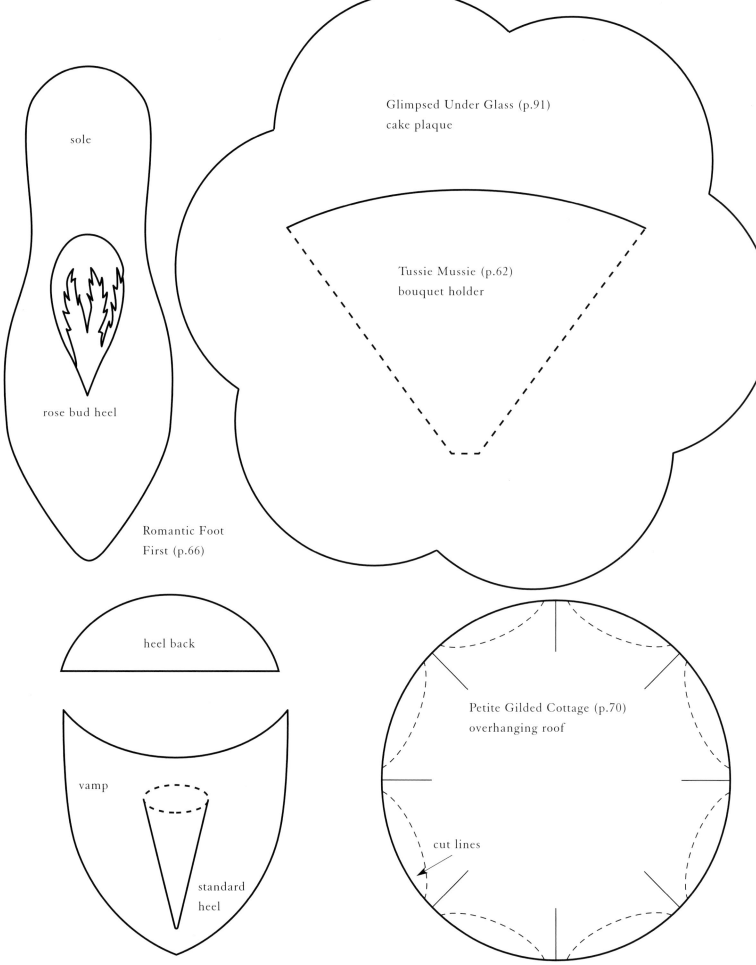

sole

rose bud heel

Romantic Foot
First (p.66)

Glimpsed Under Glass (p.91)
cake plaque

Tussie Mussie (p.62)
bouquet holder

heel back

vamp

standard
heel

Petite Gilded Cottage (p.70)
overhanging roof

cut lines

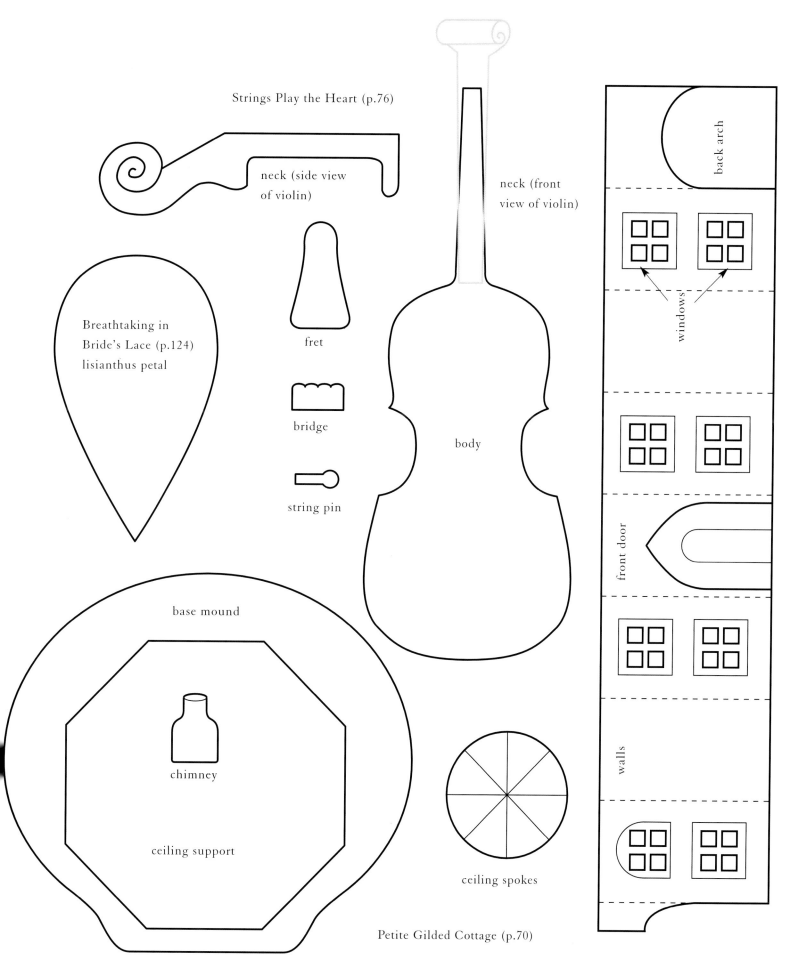

Strings Play the Heart (p.76)

neck (side view of violin)

neck (front view of violin)

back arch

windows

Breathtaking in Bride's Lace (p.124) lisianthus petal

fret

bridge

string pin

body

front door

base mound

walls

chimney

ceiling support

ceiling spokes

Petite Gilded Cottage (p.70)

155

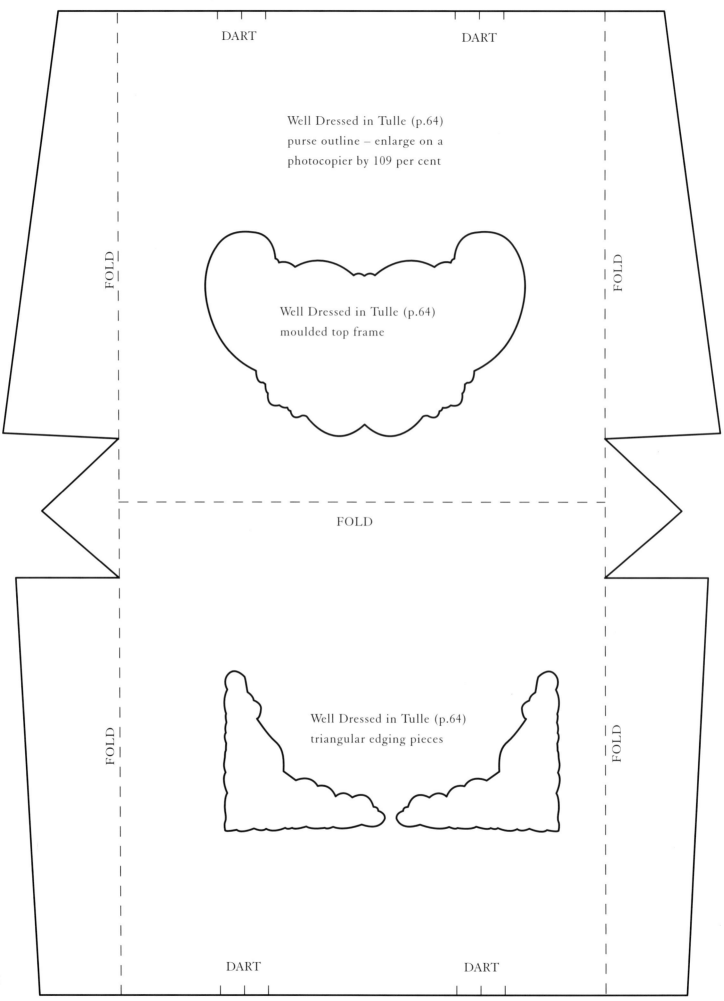

DART

DART

Well Dressed in Tulle (p.64)
purse outline – enlarge on a
photocopier by 109 per cent

FOLD

FOLD

Well Dressed in Tulle (p.64)
moulded top frame

FOLD

Well Dressed in Tulle (p.64)
triangular edging pieces

FOLD

FOLD

DART

DART

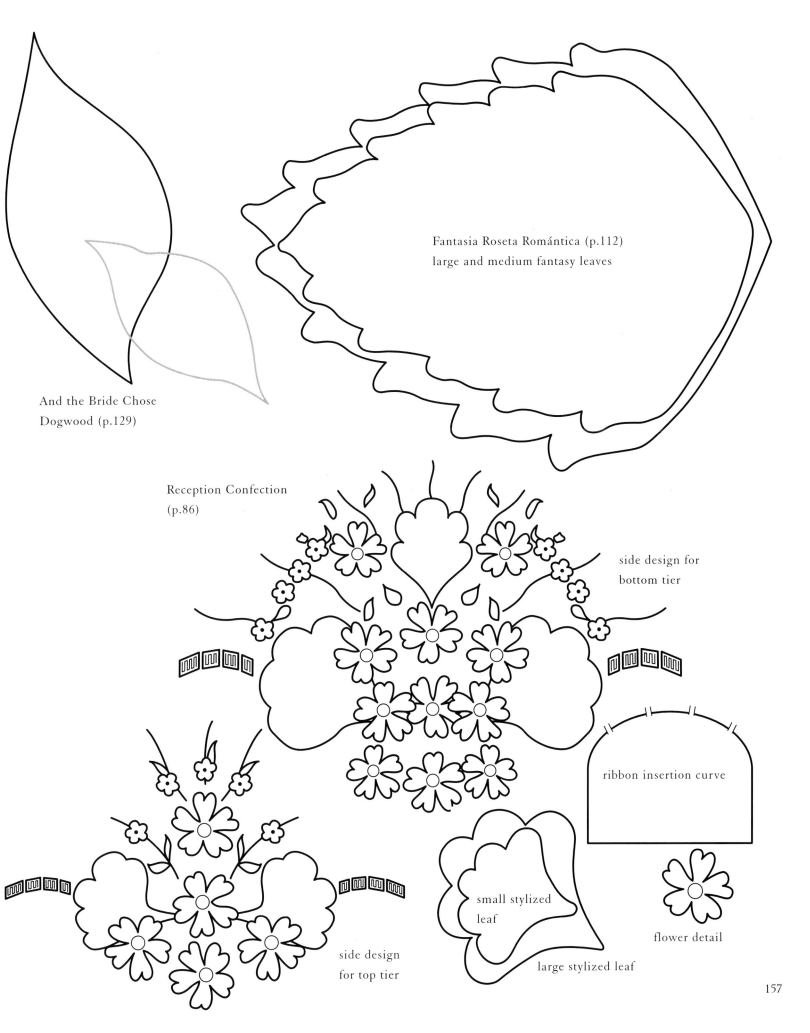

And the Bride Chose
Dogwood (p.129)

Fantasia Roseta Romántica (p.112)
large and medium fantasy leaves

Reception Confection
(p.86)

side design for
bottom tier

ribbon insertion curve

small stylized
leaf

flower detail

side design
for top tier

large stylized leaf

baroque trim for top tier
(turn pattern over for
left-hand design)

Invitation to a Summer
Wedding (p.104)

underlay for top tier

baroque trim for bottom
tier (turn pattern over
for left-hand design)

underlay for bottom tier

A Jewel in the Crown
(p.96)
filigree pattern

A Jewel in the Crown (p.96)
teardrop

Suppliers

UNITED KINGDOM

Hawthorne Hill (HH)
Milvale Studios
Milvale Street
Stoke on Trent
Staffordshire ST6 3NT
01782 811 877
(moulds)

Patchwork Cutters (PC)
3 Raines Close
Greasby, Wirral L49 2QB
0151 6785053

P.M.E. Sugarcraft (PME)
Brember Close
South Harrow
Middlesex HA2 8UN
020 8864 0888

Creative Stencil Designs
(CSD)
Flanders Moss
Station Road
Buchlyvie
Stirlingshire FK8 3NB
01360 850389

Culpitt Cake Art
Culpitt Ltd
Jubilee Industrial Estate
Ashington
Northumberland NE63 8UQ
01670 814545

Squires Kitchen (SK)
Squires House
3 Waverley Lane
Farnham, Surrey GU9 8BB
phone: 01252 711749
fax: 01252 714714

Guy, Paul & Co Ltd
Unit B4 Foundry Way
Little End Road
Eaton Socon
Cambs PE19 3JH

Vee Bee (VB)
19 Main Street (The Cross)
Kilbirnie, Ayshire KA25 7BX
0150 568 3689
(petal and lustre dusts)

Celcakes and Celcrafts (CC)
Springfield House
Gate Helmsley, York
Yorkshire T04 1NF
01759 371447

The Old Bakery (TOB/RVO)
Kingston St Mary
Taunton, Somerset TA2 8HW
phone: 01823 451 205
email: theoldbakery@
hotmail.com

Torbay Cake Craft (TCC/EC)
5 Seaway Road
Preston, Paignton
Devon TQ3 2NX
01803 550178

FMM
Unit 5, Kings Park Ind. Estate
Primrose Hill
Kings Langley
Herts WD4 8ST
phone: 01923 268699
fax: 01923 261226
email: clements@
f-m-m.demon.co.uk

Orchard Products (OP)
51 Hallyburton Road
Hove, East Sussex BN3 7GP
phone: 01273 419418
fax: 01273 412512
email: gsfashby@aol.com

British Bakels Ltd
Granville Way,
Off Launton Road
Bicester Oxon OX6 OJT
phone: 01869 247 098
fax: 01869 242 979
email:
anyone@bakels.demon.co.uk

Wilton (W)
Knightsbridge Bakeware
Centre (UK) Ltd
Chadwell Heath Lane
Romford, Essex RM6 4NP
phone: 028 590 5959
fax: 0208 590 7373
email: kbc@where.co.uk
www.cakedecoration.co.uk

UNITED STATES

Earlene Moore (EM)
1323 E. 78th
Lubbock TX 79404
email:
Earlene@earlenescakes.com

Nicholas Lodge (NL)
The International Sugar Art
Collection
6060 Mcdonough Drive
Suite D
Norcross GA 30093 1230
freephone: 1-800 662 8925
phone: 770 453 9449
fax: 770 448 9046
email: nichlodge1@aol.com

America Cake Decorating
Supplies, Inc
3100 N.W. 72nd Ave. Unit 101
Miami FL 33122
phone: 305 592 6414
fax: 305 592 6415
email: americacake@aol.com
www.yp.bellsouth.com/
americacakedecorating

Airpen
Silkpaint Corporation (SPC)
PO Box 18
Waldron, MO 64092
www.silkpaint.com
email art@silkpaint.com
freephone: 1-800 563 0074
phone: 816 4891 7774
fax: 816 891 7775

Airpen UK agent:
Suasion
35 Riding Horse Street
London W1P 7PT
phone: 020 7636 4287
email: Suasion@aol.com

Thompson's Costume
Trim & Fabric
1232 Southwest 59th Street
Oklahoma City OK 73109
phone: 405 631 8850
fax: 405 631 3450
(fabric supplier for Romantic
Table Trends)

J. Boyer
Designer Fabrics,Ltd
8142 S Harvard
Tulsa OK 74137
phone: 918 491 4776
(fabrics in this book)

Stress Free Cake Supports
Arlene House
42551 299th Street
Scotland D57059

Beryl's Cakes Decorating
P.O. Box 1584
North Springfield
VA 22151 – 0584
freephone: 1-800 4882749
fax: 703 750 3779
email: beryls@beryls.com
www.beryls.com

*All sugarpaste/rolled fondant
used in this book was
provided by*
American Bakels Inc
8114 Scott Hamilton Drive
Little Rock AR 72209
freephone: 1800 799 2253
phone: 501 568 2253
fax: 501 568 3947
email: ambakels@swbell.net
www.bakels.com

Agbay Products, Inc.
11 Hampton Street
Auburn MA 01501
phone: 508 743 5169
email: maureen@
agbayproducts.com
www.agbayproducts.com
(cake levelling tool)

John and Judy Shelton
Decotek
2108 El Camino Ave
Sacramento CA 95821
phone: 916 564 2253
fax: 916 344 3145
email: decotek@aol.com
(fondant lifter)

Darla Avra
102 West Mike
Sapulpa OK 74066
Phone: 918 227 4623
www.cakinbake.com
email:
cakinbake@cakinbake.com

Sugar Bouquets (SB)
23 North State Drive
Morristown, New Jersey 07960
freephone (US): 1-800 203
0629
phone: 973 538 3542
fax: 973 538 4939
www.sugarbouquets.com
email:
mail@sugarbouquets.com

E.M. Berling reproduction
silicone molds
Beatrice Knapik (ADM)
3 Crestview Lane
Sutton, MA 01527
508 865 2755

CK Products (CK)
310 Racquet Dr
Fort Wayne IN 46825
phone: 219 484 2517
fax: 219 484 2510
email: mail@ckproducts.com
www.ckproducts.com
(beadmakers and colours)

Vi Whittington
Country Kitchen Sweet Art
4621 Speedway Drive
Fort Wayne, IN 46825
freephone: 1-888 497 3927
email: cntryktchn@aol.com
www.countrykitchensa.com

Jack Gerber
HIS Designs (HD)
7279 Road 87
Paulding OH 45879
phone: 419 399 3535
email: hiscake@bright.net
www.weddingcakestands.com

The Dummy Place
44 Midland Drive
Tolland CT 06084
phone: 860 875 1736
email:
SLLEE@compuserve.com
(cake dummies)

Wilton Industries (W)
2240 W 75th Street
Woodbridge IL 60517
freephone: 1-800 794 5866Ö
1800 7 WILTON
freefax: 1-888 824 9520
phone: 630 963 7100
fax: 630 810 2256
email: info@wilton.com
www.wilton.com

AUSTRALIA

Major Cake Decoration
Supplies
900 Albany Highway
East Victoria Park
Western Australia 6101.
phone/fax: 618 9362 5202
Classes and equipment.

Cake & Icing Centre
651 Samford Road
Mitchelton, Queensland 4053
617 3355 3443

The Cake Decorating Centre
32-34 King William Street,
Adelaide 5000
618 8410 1944

Cake Decorating School of
Australia
Shop 7 Port Phillip Arcade
232 Flinders Street
Melbourne, VIC 3000
03 9654 5335

Cupid's Cake Decorations
2/90 Belford Street
Broadmeadow, NSW 2292
phone: 02 4962 1884
fax: 02 4961 6594

Susie Q Cake Decorating
Centre
Shop 4, 372 Keilor Road
Niddrie VIC
Australia
613 9379 2275

NEW ZEALAND

Hitchon International
220 Abtiqua Street
Christchurch
64 33653843

IRELAND

Cakes and Co
25 Rock Hill
Blackrock Village
Co. Dublin
35312836544

PERU

Rosa Viacava de Ortega (RVO)
Av. Brasil 1141 Jesus Maria
Lima 11, Peru
phone: 511 423 4210
phone/fax: 511 423 5986
email:
ortega viacava@hotmail.

ARGENTINA

Ediciones Ballina Codai SA
Av. Cordoba 2415 1st Floor
Buenos Aires
Argentina C1120AAG
54 11 4962 5381

SOUTH AFRICA

JEM Cutters (J)
P.O. Box 115 Kloof 3640
Kwazulu Natal
South Africa
0027 31 7011431
maytham@iafrica.com

Eleanor Rielander (RL)
P.O. Box 1138 Mondeor
Johannesburg 2110
South Africa

Index

First published in 2001 by Merehurst Limited
Merehurst is a Murdoch Books (UK) Ltd imprint

ISBN 1-85391-810 5
A catalogue record of this book is available from the
British Library.

Text copyright © Kerry Vincent 2001
Photography copyright © Merehurst Limited
Kerry Vincent has asserted her right under the
Copyright, Designs and Patents Act, 1988.

Commissioning Editor: Barbara Croxford
Project Editor: Joanna Chisholm
Designer: Maggie Aldred
Photography: Hawks photography, Oklahoma, USA

CEO: Robert Oerton
Publisher: Catie Ziller
Publishing Manager: Fia Fornari
Production Manager: Lucy Byrne

Group General Manager: Mark Smith
Group CEO/Publisher: Anne Wilson

Colour separation by Colourscan, Singapore

Printed by Tien Wah Press, Singapore

Murdoch Books (UK) Ltd
Ferry House, 51–57 Lacy Road,
Putney, London SW15 1PR
Tel: +44 (0)20 8355 1480, Fax: +44 (0)20 8355 1499
Murdoch Books (UK) Ltd is a subsidiary of
Murdoch Magazines Pty Ltd

Murdoch Books
GPO Box 1203
Sydney, Australia, NSW 1045
Tel: +61 (0)2 9692 2347 Fax: +61 (0)2 9692 2559

Murdoch Books is a trademark of Murdoch
Magazines Pty Ltd